PeaceTalk

PeaceTalk

A Compendium of Hope

LEO R. SANDY
RAY PERKINS
ASHLEY L. GREENE

Foreword by Thomas F. Lee

WIPF & STOCK · Eugene, Oregon

Wipf & Stock
An Imprint of Wipf and Stock Publishers
199 W. 8th Ave., Suite 3
Eugene, OR 97401

www.wipfandstock.com

PAPERBACK ISBN: 979-8-3852-3406-6
HARDCOVER ISBN: 979-8-3852-3407-3
EBOOK ISBN: 979-8-3852-3408-0

Scripture quotations marked (ESV) are taken from The Holy Bible, English Standard Version®, Copyright© 2001 by Crossway, a publishing ministry of Good News Publishers. Used by permission.

Scripture quotations marked (KJV) are taken from the King James Version, public domain.

Scripture quotations marked (NKJV) are taken from the New King James Version®. Copyright© 1982 by Thomas Nelson, Inc. Used by permission. All rights reserved.

Scripture quotations marked (NRSV) are taken from the New Revised Standard Version Bible, © 1989 the Division of Christian Education of the National Council of the Churches of Christ in the United States of America. Used by permission. All rights reserved.

09/18/25

"In an age where global conflicts continue to dominate head-lines—from ongoing wars in Eastern Europe and the Middle East to civil unrest and humanitarian crises—the need for a collective rethinking of our response to violence has never been greater. *PeaceTalk* not only challenges the deeply ingrained belief that war is inevitable, but also offers practical, philosophical, and educational pathways to nurturing a culture of peace.

"What makes this book especially relevant for today . . . is its bold assertion that war is not inherent to human nature but is instead a conditioned behavior, deeply embedded through social structures and reinforced by language and training. . . . This reflection calls for educators, psychologists, and peace practitioners to address the root causes of violence not just through conflict resolution, but through a complete transformation of how societies define heroism, nationalism, and conflict.

"The authors' concept of battlebabble, as introduced by Thomas F. Lee, powerfully illustrates how language is weaponized to normalize militarism and glorify war. . . . [It is important] to help learners become critical thinkers who can decode such language and replace it with what this book so aptly calls peacetalk—language grounded in justice, dignity, and nonviolence. Peace education, then, becomes not just a subject, but a way of seeing, questioning, and reshaping the world. . . . In a world on the edge of ecological and nuclear catastrophe, *PeaceTalk* does not just provide knowledge—it provides hope and a call to action."

—AFSHAN HUMA, Assistant Professor, Educational Planning, Policy Studies, and Leadership, Allama Iqbal Open University, Pakistan

We dedicate this book to renowned philosopher, Bertrand Russell (1872–1970); scholar of nonviolence and the founder of the Albert Einstein Institution, Gene Sharp (1928–2018); Marine combat veteran and cofounder of Veterans for Peace, Inc., Col. John Barr (1924–2014); and to all people who dedicate their lives to peace, social justice, nonviolence, and the abolition of war.

Contents

Foreword

WARS ARE SYNONYMOUS WITH the history of humanity. These violent conflicts between nations and neighbors are too often thought of as inevitable. Long before the tragic events of our current war-torn era, the complex web of biological instincts, learned behaviors, and psychological undercurrents that make up a human being have allowed a kind of conditioning to take place, convincing humans to battle to the death and call it a noble act. Young men and women, while anxiously reluctant to do what their instincts tell them is wrong, act out what their training has conditioned them to do—kill and maim whomever their government and superiors identify as the enemy.

However, war, despite its distressing frequency and violence, is not natural to humans. It is estimated that during World War II almost every combatant, if they escaped death or wounds, would ultimately break down after 200 to 240 days in combat, unable to go on. That is why new recruits must be isolated for at least six to twelve weeks of "basic training" where they are conditioned by methods honed over centuries to form cohesive units who will kill on command.[1]

And yet, despite this gruesome practice, modern societies so often elevate the notion of war to a glorious "struggle" to achieve "victory" measured with the bodies of the dead. History buffs reenact famous battles of the American Civil War—a vicious, protracted struggle in which over 620,000 soldiers died—more

1. See Lee, *Battlebabble.*

than in both world wars, Korea, Vietnam, Afghanistan, and Iraq. Moreover, since the horrors of Hiroshima and Nagasaki in 1945, in which over 100,000 Japanese were incinerated by atomic bombs and many thousands more were injured, vastly more powerful nuclear weapons have been developed. Nine nations, principally Russia and the United States, now possess a total global nuclear warhead inventory of 13,400, many of which are primed for release within minutes. Beyond these fearsome weapons of mass destruction, there is an alarming growth of inexpensive and effective weapons systems—armed drones and robots—that can lead to crippling attacks by lesser actors. It should be obvious that we must somehow turn away from this sad history and the ongoing threat of mutual destruction. We must abolish war, or it will abolish us.[2]

But how will that come about? This book is a determined effort to guide the efforts of peacemakers—people dedicated to peace, social justice, and nonviolent solutions to conflicts. Peace studies programs are proliferating in which a multitude of new, specific approaches to the mitigation and abolition of war are sought. The students and practitioners in those programs, working on what this important book calls "peacefixing," will find valuable information and inspiration here.

The authors have called on their years of experience in a wide variety of relevant disciplines, including history, philosophy, psychology, peace studies, Holocaust and genocide studies, and human development. They have taught at the college or university level for a combined total of over sixty years, publishing widely on peace matters, and have been active participants in peace-promoting organizations. One, Leo Sandy, is a Navy veteran.

I am grateful that this volume follows and complements my 2005 book *Battlebabble: Selling War in America*. The deceptive language that I recount in my dictionary of deception employed to support and promote militarism has serious and deadly consequences. *PeaceTalk: A Compendium of Hope* will guide readers in their search for effective, alternative pathways and innovative

2. See Kristensen et al., "World Nuclear Forces."

strategies towards a world where nonviolence, reconciliation, and peace are seen as the first logical and effective choices, rather than the ravages of war.

—THOMAS F. LEE, PHD

Acknowledgments

WE WOULD LIKE TO acknowledge the following for their assistance: Shakti Maira on Hinduism, Dawn C. Berry on Christianity, Gary Goodnough and Ron Maurno on Judaism, and Rubina Tariq on Islam. We would also like to thank the Keene State College students who provided feedback on early drafts of the book as part of their coursework in peace studies.

Introduction

The end of war and international violence is a fundamental requirement for victory of the human spirit.

—JOHN NORTON MOORE, CHAIRMAN, US INSTITUTE OF PEACE, BIENNIAL REPORT TO CONGRESS, 1989

THIS BOOK WAS INSPIRED by Thomas Lee's *Battlebabble* (2005)—a poignant book that brings home the power of government and media to use language to sell the public on the notion that war is necessary and even good. Lee was mainly concerned with the 2003 US war against Iraq. In hindsight, it seems incredible that the American people could have been so easily persuaded to do the business of what now is almost universally perceived as a tragic and shameful mistake. That persuasion was accomplished largely with the help of official "battlebabble," which Lee recounts in a dictionary of pro-war doublespeak taken from American media and the Pentagon. This battlebabble, Lee argues, fed a national mania seemingly incapable of critical thought and enamored with "shock and awe." Thus, Americans and Iraqis were plunged into more than two decades of war and political upheaval from which the region has yet to fully emerge.

War, we are told, has been with us for millennia and will be with us forever—an inescapable facet of human nature. Of course, the same has been said of many institutions we now hold in contempt, including the legal enslavement of human beings and the denial of women's suffrage. But apart from the perennial controversy concerning the nature of human nature, two things seem clear:

1. despite the so-called inexorable laws of tradition and human nature, people have time and again demonstrated the collective power to change cultural institutions that clear thinking and moral sense revealed to be in need of change; and

2. in the case of war, if people don't make changes to this deadly institution, war will almost certainly shape, perhaps even end, our world as we know it.

The first proposition seems incontestable, a plain fact of human history. But of course, the second proposition could be, and has been, cast in doubt, either as alarmist or as too remote a possibility to warrant immediate concern. The uncomfortable truth is that despite the end of the Cold War, we are not out of the nuclear woods yet. It would take only a fraction of the world's approximately twelve thousand remaining nuclear weapons to instantly kill tens of millions of people and potentially plunge the planet into a nuclear winter in which billions would die of starvation. And surely, given enough time and a world with many more nuclear-armed nations, the use of nuclear weapons—through accident, terrorism, madness, or miscalculation—becomes a near mathematical certainty.

One of the most insidious consequences of battlebabble is that it distracts us from these two propositions, both the ability of people to alter even the most entrenched institutions and the imperative of finding alternatives to war. The chief merit of Lee's book was to show us the irrationality and potency of war culture and its language. Thus, language can be used to both reveal and obfuscate the truth. But seeing battlebabble for what it is—a culture stoked to breed fear and designed to convince us that responding to conflict with violence is both rational and inevitable—we are free to imagine a culture based on alternative presumptions, free to think and talk about alternatives to war. We call this discussion "peace talk." We also think of our book as a natural sequel to Lee's *Battlebabble* and a valuable guide to understanding and promoting a culture of peace.

The culture of peace is a culture every bit as old as the culture of war, but until recently its story has been drowned out by the culture of war and its incessant babble. In fact, it could be argued that the world only began to see the need and possibilities for collective action for peace in the last century, and especially since World War II. That war did several things to foster a culture of peace. The loss of sixty million lives (six times the casualties experienced during the First World War) brought the horrors of war into homes and families around the world.[3] And although the crime that would later come to be known as genocide had occurred many times before the Second World War, the Nazis' systematic attempt to exterminate European Jews exposed the dangers of unchecked militarism and exclusionary ideology in a way that demanded global attention. World War II also introduced a new technology for waging war—the atomic bomb. For the first time in human history, we had the means to exterminate our own species. These stark realities prompted Albert Einstein to remark, "The unleashed power of the atom has changed everything except our ways of thinking, and thus we drift toward unparalleled catastrophe."[4] Einstein (and other peacemakers discussed in chapter 2 saw that the long-term survival of humanity required new ways of thinking—ways which could envision alternatives to war and the relationships, structures, and systems that undermine peace and human security.

New ways of thinking and strategies for nonviolent solutions to international problems have indeed emerged and are operating across the planet. With the end of World War II in 1945, nations around the world came together in an unprecedented alliance to form the United Nations (UN). In its founding charter, the UN pledged to advance four primary goals:

1. to take effective, collective action to maintain international security and prevent threats to peace;

2. to make respect for equal rights the basis of friendly relations among nations;

3. National WWII Museum, "Cost of War."
4. Holt, "Meet Einstein's Challenge."

3. to promote human rights and fundamental freedoms for all people regardless of their identity, and to cooperate in solving international problems, be they economic, social, cultural, or humanitarian; and

4. to harmonize the actions of its member nations "in the attainment of these common ends."[5]

Today the UN boasts 193 member states. While not perfect in implementation or results, UN humanitarian efforts reach all corners of the globe. They have provided food to some ninety million people in seventy-three countries; vaccinated nearly 60 percent of the world's children; maintained 122,000 peacekeepers in sixteen countries on four continents; and assisted more than thirty-six million refugees and people fleeing war and persecution.[6]

Following the birth of the UN, many of the world's governments signed declarations recognizing rights and freedoms that should be common and protected for all. The 1948 Universal Declaration of Human Rights affirmed, among other rights, the right of all peoples to be free from enslavement, from arbitrary detention, to enjoy freedom of movement within the borders of their country, and to seek asylum from persecution in countries not their own. That same year, the UN General Assembly unanimously adopted the Convention on the Prevention and Punishment of Genocide. The Convention became international law in 1951.

World leaders began collaborating on issues of global concern. After a tense standoff between the US and the Soviet Union during the 1962 Cuban Missile Crisis, nations turned in earnest to agreements that would advance nuclear arms control. The Limited Test Ban Treaty of 1963 and The Comprehensive Test Ban Treaty of 1998 outlawed nuclear testing. The 1968 Nuclear Non-Proliferation Treaty (NPT) and the Strategic Arms Reduction Treaties (START) (1991 and 2011) reduced global nuclear stockpiles, lowering the number of nuclear weapons from sixty thousand in 1980 to fewer than thirteen thousand today. Ninety-seven percent

5. UN, "United Nations Charter."
6. Mortimer, "First 70 Years."

of the world's governments have signed onto the NPT and thanks to these treaties, there are only nine nuclear weapons states today instead of the dozens that American President John F. Kennedy predicted by the end of the twentieth century. And while outliers such as North Korea continue to pursue nuclear weapons, the fact that the majority of the world's nations have agreed to disarm is a milestone in humanity's march toward a more secure future.

Advancements in our understanding of the causes of war and conflict represent another pivotal step in our planet's progress toward peace. Peace studies is now a flourishing field with academics and practitioners working to develop best practices for conflict transformation and for the advancement of positive peace—peace that goes beyond the absence of war to address the systemic inequalities that underpin societal institutions and prevent people from receiving equal access to needs and opportunities (structural violence). Programs for peace studies, conflict resolution, and genocide studies exist around the world, preparing students for careers in international policy, mediation, disaster relief, law, development work, and education, to name a few.

The world has also learned much about preventing violence before it happens. Sophisticated early warning systems blend qualitative and quantitative data to assess the impact of risk factors—from regime type to weather patterns—on societies' level of vulnerability to conflict and identity-based crimes like genocide. Based on these indicators of risk, policymakers, members of civil society, and academics are working together to develop innovative models for prevention and early response.[7]

And of course, underpinning academic and policy achievements are extraordinary individuals who have resisted oppression and championed human rights at great risk and personal cost. Nelson Mandela emerged from twenty-seven years in prison to lead post-Apartheid South Africa out of racial segregation and into a period of democracy and reconciliation. Born a slave in nineteenth-century New York, Sojourner Truth escaped with

---

7. For examples, see Waller, *Confronting Evil*, and Greene and Sentongo, "Assessing National Mechanisms."

her infant daughter to become a leading figure in the American abolitionist and women's rights movements. Thich Nhat Hahn defied the norms of the Buddhist monastery in Vietnam to develop the Plum Village Tradition, where monks worked directly within communities. His work inspired a social movement known as "engaged Buddhism," which applies Buddhist ethics and mediation practices to issues of suffering and injustice. Across the planet, the actions of people dedicated to a more just world have toppled dictators, challenged systems of oppression, and led movements both local and global to transform conflict and advance social and economic justice.

Observers of world events will note that we are still a long way from realizing the peacebuilding potential envisioned by the architects of the UN. Inequalities remain within and across societies, people continue to be persecuted on the basis of their collective identity, and missed opportunities for early intervention, expanded collaboration, de-escalation, and military reduction abound. As we write this book, wars or major crises persist in Democratic Republic of Congo, Haiti, Myanmar, Sudan, the Middle East, and Eastern Europe; sadly this is a representative rather than exhaustive list. Yet for all their shortcomings, the aforementioned efforts to advance peace and security represent a shared commitment to exploring new ways of thinking and new strategies that diminish the need for war and promote universal flourishing. In so doing, they offer us an opportunity to arrest the drift toward catastrophe that Einstein foresaw for humanity.

In the pages that follow, readers will encounter the ideas, individuals, and organizations that have shaped what is now a vibrant and sophisticated field dedicated to understanding the causes of conflict and advancing positive peace. In chapter 1, we provide a dictionary of terms related to the study of peace, with suggested readings for students who wish to delve further. Chapter 2 is dedicated to individuals, past and present, who have championed peace in their societies and shaped the contours of the field. Chapter 3 discusses some notable peacemaking organizations, including organizations dedicated specifically to veterans and the individuals (nurses, fighter pilots, foot soldiers, etc.) whose experiences of war have fueled their advocacy for peace. Chapter 4 gives the interested student and educator information about some of the rapidly growing peace studies programs and publications around the world. In chapter 5, we briefly discuss major world religions and describe some of their beliefs and practices that contribute to a culture of peace. Finally, in chapter 6 we offer suggestions for tackling some of the current problems that need some "peacefixing"[8] so that a culture of peace can continue to grow and war can be abolished. Over the last century the human condition worldwide has improved by several measures known to be relevant to the promotion of peace. These include significant increases globally in literacy, the education of women, democratic governments, human health, per capita income, population stability, and significant reductions in the number of interstate wars and military casualties. We hope that the readers and students who pick up this book will be inspired by these successes and will add innovative strategies of their own to the world's quest for peace.

8. For "peacefixing," see Owen, *Mortification of Sin* where the term is used to refer to attempts at making peace.

1

A Definition of Terms

ABOLISH WAR CAMPAIGN

THE ABOLISH WAR CAMPAIGN was launched by retired US Marine Corps Col. John Barr at the 1987, second annual Veterans For Peace Convention. Barr served in the military for thirty years, participating in combat in Korea and Vietnam and retiring in 1973 after refusing a promotion to the rank of general. Barr worked for ten years as a nuclear weapons employment officer. After retiring from the military, he become an outspoken critic of the nuclear arms race. He believed the existence of nuclear weapons in the hands of a few men was a new and insidious form of tyranny. Modern weapons could no longer be used to resolve conflicts with sanity, he argued.

The abolition of war became a central aim of Veterans For Peace. Barr promoted the campaign by delivering anti-war messages at colleges and institutions across New England. He was known to show up with a briefcase on which he taped a note: "This briefcase contains radioactive material. It could blow up your whole city." Barr used the ploy as a conversation starter about the dangers of nuclear warfare. Those familiar with Barr came to recognize the "EndWar" license plate on his car and the Abolish War Campaign's bumper stickers which read: "Abolish War—it's the only option!"[1]

In 1995 Barr wrote an unpublished manuscript titled "We Are Abolishing War." In it, he provided arguments against war taken from citizen testimony, military admonitions, religious roots, and the arts. He also traced myths about war, outlined impediments to ending war, and discussed organizational, political, and other strategic initiatives to abolish war. "The concepts are evolved; the institutions are in place; the laws are duly enacted; it remains only to consolidate the will," Barr wrote.[2]

The Abolish War Campaign represented a growing group of military veterans taking an active role in America's anti-war movement. It engaged with what David P. Barash has called "the most fundamental struggle" in abolishing war—"to challenge war itself, the social and political process of mass killing in the name of the state, for the sake of wealth and power, in defense of ideology and a way of life, allegedly on behalf of security in self-defense, but also to satisfy expansionist ambitions."[3] After Barr's death in 2014, his daughter found a neatly typed index card in his papers. "War is obsolete," it said. "The survival of humanity depends on its ability to mature and learn to resolve conflicts without violence."[4]

Suggested Reading

Veterans for Peace. "Who We Are." https://www.veteransforpeace.org/who-we-are.

1. Genesio, *Veterans for Peace*, 242.
2. Barr, "We Are Abolishing War."
3. Barash, *Approaches to Peace*, 252.
4. Ely, "Remembrance Project."

AHIMSA

True ahimsa should mean a complete freedom from ill-will
and anger and hate and an overflowing love for all.

—Mahatma Gandhi

Ahimsa, a Sanskrit word that translates literally to non-harm, is
best known as a central component of Mahatma Gandhi's philosophy of nonviolence, though it is also an important virtue in Hinduism, Jainism, Buddhism, and Sikhism. Gandhi saw *ahimsa* as the
complete rejection of violence, anger, and hate in word, thought,
and deed. Under *ahimsa*, Gandhi argued, there is no room for assassination or murder.

> There is no room for any violence even for the sake of
> your country, and even for guarding the honor of pre-
> cious ones that may be under your charge. After all,
> that would be a poor defense of honor. The doctrine of
> *ahimsa* tells us that we may guard the honor of those
> under our charge by delivering ourselves into the hands
> of the man who would commit the sacrilege. And that
> requires far greater physical and mental courage than the
> delivering of blows.[5]

While Gandhi saw *ahimsa* as a goal that required continual work
and discipline to achieve, he believed it had the power to end
cycles of violence and transform relationships. *Ahimsa* became
a critical component of Gandhi's strategy of noncooperation
and civil disobedience, which he used to resist racial restrictions
against Asians in South Africa and achieve political independence
for India without firing a shot. Gandhi's incorporation of *ahimsa*
into a strategy for achieving large-scale social and political change
has influenced nonviolent movements around the world. Gandhi
wrote, "They say 'means are [just] means.' I would say, 'means are
after all everything.' As the means, so the end."[6]

5. Cortright, *Truth Seekers*, 14.
6. Cortright, *Truth Seekers*, 12.

Suggested Reading

Cortright, David, ed. *Truth Seekers: Voices of Peace and Nonviolence from Gandhi to Pope Francis.* Maryknoll, NY: Orbis, 2020.

ANATOMY OF PEACE

Anatomy of Peace, by Emery Reves, is among the most influential books written on the topic of ending war in the wake of World War II. Published in 1945, it advocated for world federalism—a system in which a world government, based on law, would govern the intergovernmental relationships of sovereign nation states. Reves, a Hungarian Jew, was a journalist and literary agent to Winston Churchill. He believed that bodies such as the League of Nations (and its successor the UN) would always be instruments of power, while nothing short of an instrument of world law would be able to preserve peace between nations. *Anatomy of Peace* remained on the *New York Times* bestseller list for six months. By 1950, it had appeared in twenty languages in twenty-four countries, making it a canonical text in the world governance movement.[7]

Suggested Reading

Crockatt, Richard. "World Government." In *Einstein and Twentieth-Century Politics: "Salutary Moral Influence,"* 133–37. Oxford: Oxford University Press, 2016.

Reves, Emery. *The Anatomy of Peace*. Special ed. Dallas: Dallas Symphony Association, 1994.

ANIMAL RIGHTS

There is little that separates humans from other sentient beings—we all feel joy, we all deeply crave to be alive and to live freely, and we all share this planet together.

—MAHATMA GANDHI

7. Molineu, Review of *One World*.

4

The history of animal rights stretches far into the human past—as far at least as the sixth century BCE when Pythagoras put forward the first known argument in favor of vegetarianism. In 1683, the Christian theologian Thomas Tyron wrote the first publication in the English language to associate the term "rights" with animals. And in 1789, Jeremy Bentham advocated for the humane treatment of animals as sentient beings with a dictum that would later influence key thinkers of the modern human rights movement: "The question is not, Can they *reason*? Nor, Can they *talk*? But, Can they *suffer*?"[8]

Proponents of animal rights have a history of influencing and being influenced by the advancement of human rights. In Europe, female authors such as Margaret Cavendish (1623–1673) and Francis Power Cobbe (1822–1904) drew links between the mistreatment of animals and the abuse of women to criticize male brutality and societal inequalities like the inability of women to vote. Cobbe's 1878 article, "Wife-Torture in England," condemned the abuse of women and the practice of vivisection-experimentation on the nerves of living dogs. The late nineteenth and twentieth century saw a proliferation of social movements that saw themselves as fighting against cruelty of all kinds, whether to humans or animals. The Humanitarian League, begun by Henry Salt in 1891, had an eclectic mission that ranged from criminal and prison law reform to animal cruelty in slaughterhouses, blood sports, and the trade in feathers. Salt believed that "The emancipation of . . . [humans] from cruelty and injustice will bring with it in due course the emancipation of animals also. The two reforms are inseparably connected, and neither can be fully realized alone."[9] In his fight for social and political change, Gandhi, who credited his decision to become a vegetarian to Salt's influence, advocated fiercely for the doctrine of *ahimsa*—the cornerstone of Hindu ethics that demands non-harm towards all living beings.

The close connection between animal rights and human rights continued into the modern animal rights movement,

8. Munro, *Cruelest Animal*, 18.
9. Nibert, *Animal Rights*, 236.

commonly marked by the publication of Peter Singer's book *Animal Liberation: A New Ethic for Our Treatment of Animals* in 1975. In their co-authored book published the following year, *Animal Rights and Human Obligations*, Singer and Tom Regan connected the abuse of animals—which they saw as a form of speciesism—to racism and prejudices against people. A final example is the 2002 work, *Animal Rights/Human Rights: Entanglements of Oppression and Liberation*, by sociologist David Nibert. Nibert traced the a history of civilization in which the oppression of animals has gone hand-in-hand with the oppression of human beings, each perpetuating the other. He locates the causes of both types of oppression in structures of prejudice that have been driven by economics and elites, legitimated through ideology, and protected by state power. Like Salt, Nibert argued that efforts to end human oppression will inevitably be deeply entangled with efforts to stop the oppression of animals. His work suggested that "the liberation of devalued groups of humans is unlikely in a world that uses other animals as fodder for the continual growth and expansion of transnational corporations and, conversely, that animal liberation cannot take place when humans continue to be exploited and oppressed."[10]

Suggested Reading

Nibert, David. *AnimalRights/Human Rights: Entanglements of Oppression and Liberation.* Lanham, MD: Rowman & Littlefield, 2002.
Munro, Lyle. *Man Is the Cruelest Animal: Essays on the Human-Animal Link.* Champaign, IL: Common Ground Research Networks, 2021.

ARAB SPRING

In the spring of 2011, a series of pro-democracy uprisings swept several largely Muslim countries, including Tunisia, Syria, Morocco, Egypt, Libya, and Bahrain. The uprisings were inspired by Mohammed Bouazizi, a Tunisian street vendor who set himself on fire in December 2010 to protest the arbitrary seizing of his vegetable

10. See Nibert, *Animal Rights/Human Rights.*

stand by police. The peaceful demonstrations that followed in the streets of Tunis led authoritarian president Zine El Abidine Ben Ali to peacefully abdicate his position after ruling for more than twenty years. Tunisia's success was a catalyst for grassroots movements across the region seeking political and social change. The protests had a lasting impact on the Middle East and northern Africa. In Tunisia, Egypt, and Libya they led to regime changes. In some cases, governments met the protests with brutal force and oppression, escalating to civil wars in Libya, Syria, and Yemen. The Arab Spring exemplifies both the power of nonviolent action and the tremendous challenges facing pro-democracy movements in authoritarian countries.

Suggested Reading

Blaydes, Lisa, et al. *Struggles for Political Change in the Arab World: Regimes, Oppositions, and External Actors After the Spring.* Ann Arbor: University of Michigan Press, 2022.

ARMS CONTROL

Arms control refers to any international agreement that limits or prohibits the testing, development, or use of weapons. Arms control aims to prevent the outbreak of war or to limit its destructiveness if prevention fails. While the practice of placing limits on weaponry is not modern—the Roman Catholic Church banned Christians from using crossbows against other Christians in the Second Lateran Council of 1139[11]—the strategy entered the modern international arena with the 1899 and 1907 Hague Conventions, which sought to prohibit the use of asphyxiating gases and certain types of ammunition such as expanding bullets. This began a series of arms-control agreements, including the Washington Conference (1921–1922) and the Geneva Protocols (1925), the latter of which banned countries from using chemical and biological weapons to initiate an attack on another state. Later, the

11. History Skills, "Church Declare a Ban."

1972 Biological Weapons Convention and 1993 Chemical Weapons Convention added bans on the development, production, or stockpiling of such weaponry.

In some cases, individual countries sign arms control agreements to de-escalate arms races and hostilities. During the height of the Cold War, the US and the Soviet Union signed the 1972 Anti-Ballistic Missile (ABM) Treaty prohibiting nationwide, anti-ballistic missile defense systems and forbidding the testing and deployment of space-based systems. The treaty was based on the idea that limiting defense systems would prevent the need to develop more advanced offensive missile technologies. Washington and Moscow also reasoned that neither country would launch a nuclear attack on the other if they remained vulnerable to a counterattack. The treaty marked an effort to slow the nuclear arms race through the military doctrine of mutually assured destruction (MAD) and made possible a gradual reduction of nuclear arms over the next twenty years as well as the prevention of an arms race in space. It also accomplished gains toward disarmament and denuclearization. Since the end of the Cold War, the US and Russia have reduced their nuclear stockpiles by approximately 75 percent and destroyed more than forty thousand nuclear weapons.

Arms control represents a realpolitik approach to the reduction of war and its consequences. Recognizing that sovereign states act according to perceived self-interests, advocates of arms control generally view the achievement of world peace and total disarmament as unrealistic, focusing instead on immediate concessions states can reach to limit war's means and deadliness. While international arms control agreements have not been perfectly followed, they provide a starting place for nations to place restrictions on how they prepare for and conduct war.

Suggested Reading

Arms Control Association. *Arms Control Today: The Monthly Journal on Nonproliferation and Global Security.* https://www.armscontrol.org/aca/2153.

Krepon, Michael. *Winning and Losing the Nuclear Peace*. Stanford: Stanford University Press, 2021.

ATLANTIC CHARTER

During World War II, following four days of talks aboard warships, US president Franklin D. Roosevelt and British prime minister Winston Churchill issued a joint declaration on August 14, 1941 asserting eight common principles for a more peaceful future, which are summarized below:

1. Neither nation sought territorial or other aggrandizement.

2. They desired no territorial changes without the freely expressed wishes of the peoples concerned.

3. They respected peoples' right to choose their own form of government and desired the restoration of sovereign rights and self-government to those who had been forcibly deprived of them.

4. They would try to advance equal access for all nations to trade and to raw materials.

5. They would seek collaboration between nations to improve labor standards, economic advancement, and social security.

6. After the final destruction of Nazi tyranny, they would seek a peace that allowed all people to live safely and freely within their boundaries, without fear or want.

7. Such a peace would include freedom to traverse the world's seas.

8. With the establishment of a permanent system of general security, all nations should pursue disarmament and abandon the use of force or aggression against other states.[12]

By January 1942, twenty-six Allied nations had pledged support for the Atlantic Charter. Its main ideas were infused into the

---

12. See NATO, "'Atlantic Charter.'"

UN and referenced in the UN founding Charter. Decades later, the Atlantic Charter continued to inspire nations and peoples, including South African reformer and Nobel Peace Prize recipient Nelson Mandela. In his autobiography, Mandela wrote,

> Some in the West saw the charter as empty promises, but not those of us in Africa. Inspired by the Atlantic Charter and the fight of the Allies against tyranny and aggression, the ANC [the African National Congress] created its own charter called African Claims, which called for full citizenship for all Africans, the right to buy land and the repeal of all discriminating legislation.[13]

Suggested Reading

History.com. "Atlantic Charter." https://www.history.com/articles/atlantic-charter.

BASTIAT'S PRINCIPLE

A principle named after Frédéric Bastiat (1801–1850)—a French political economist who succinctly explained the connection between international trade and international peace—states that "when goods do not cross borders, soldiers will."[14] Bastiat's Principle represents a critique of protectionism—the shielding of domestic industries against foreign competition through tariffs, import quotas, or subsidies. Bastiat believed government's sole responsibility was to protect individual liberties and warned against the unseen consequences of government policy. He was a fierce champion of free markets and unrestricted international trade—once mocking protectionist policies with a satirical petition to protect the livelihood of French candlemakers from the competition of the sun by blocking its light.

13. Sands, *Lawless World*, 9.
14. OLL, "Did Bastiat Say."

Suggested Reading

Boudreaux, Donald J. "A Reflection on Bastiat's 'What Is Seen and What Is Not Seen.'" American Institute for Economic Research, Sept. 13, 2022. https://www.aier.org/article/a-reflection-on-bastiats-what-is-seen-and-what-is-not-seen/.

Online Library of Liberty. "A Reader's Guide to the Works of Frédéric Bastiat (1801–1850)." https://oll.libertyfund.org/pages/fb-readersguide.

CIVIL DISOBEDIENCE

Civil disobedience, based on an article published in 1849 by Henry David Thoreau, is a tactic and philosophy of nonviolent action that seeks to effect change by violating a law that is deemed to be unjust. Gandhi, influenced by Thoreau, was perhaps the most famous practitioner of civil disobedience—using it effectively to win independence for India from Great Britain at the end of World War II after more than thirty years of nonviolent struggle. British philosopher Bertrand Russell used civil disobedience to bring public attention to the danger of nuclear weapons, about which he believed the government was untruthful. In 1961, his arrest (at the age of eighty-nine) and week-long imprisonment for protesting garnered significant international media attention; he would later use the strategy again to protest the Vietnam War. In the US, Martin Luther King Jr. used civil disobedience to change laws of racial discrimination in the American South in the early 1960s. Following his arrest for leading an illegal march in protest of Alabama's segregation laws, King wrote his 1963 "Letter from a Birmingham Jail," articulating the principles of civil disobedience. According to King, civil disobedience must be done thoughtfully and openly and with no malice of thought toward the system of law or its lawmakers. It must be nonviolent and with a cooperative willingness to accept the penalty mandated by the legal system. Civil disobedience has been employed by movements and activists across the globe in struggles for women's rights, economic equality, environmental reform, and anti-war efforts.

Suggested Reading

King, Martin Luther, Jr. "Letter from a Birmingham Jail." Bill of Rights Institute. https://bri-wp-images.s3.amazonaws.com/wp-content/uploads/Letter-From-Birmingham-Jail.pdf.

Thoreau, Henry David. *On the Duty of Civil Disobedience.* Cranbury, NJ: Elegant Ebooks, 1849.

CIVILIAN-BASED DEFENSE (SEE OUR SECTION "TRANSARMAMENT")

The concept of civilian-based defense—a defense policy utilizing prepared civilian struggle and nonviolent action to preserve a society's freedom and sovereignty against attack—was developed by the American political scientist Gene Sharp. In his 1990 book by the same title, Sharp wrote, "Two things are certain about the future of politics and international relations: conflict is inevitable, and effective defense will be required against internal usurpers and international aggressors."[15] While Sharp believed in the inevitability of war, he was committed to nonviolence and saw it as an effective tool for defense and deterrence. He argued that violent occupations require the cooperation and control of civilian populations in order to succeed. The strategy of civilian-based defense holds that with training and strict discipline, the populations and institutions of threatened states could employ selective and mass-scale noncooperation to prevent attackers from achieving their objectives and avoid violent conflict. Entities that employ violence often expect a violent response and are prepared to deal with it. A nonviolent response, however, surprises and disrupts the aggressor and it is often ill-equipped to cope with it in a manner that serves its interests.

Suggested Reading

Sharp, Gene. *Civilian-Based Defense: A Post-Military Defense System.* Princeton: Princeton University Press, 1990.

15. Sharp, *Civilian-Based Defense*, 3.

CONFLICT RESOLUTION

Conflict resolution is an area of scholarship and professional practice focused on negotiated endings to armed conflict. Situated within the field of peace research, conflict resolution encompasses strategies for how warring parties can seek common solutions and arrive at agreements, best practices for implementing such agreements in ways that lead to durable peace, and quantitative and qualitative analyses of peace agreements. As Peter Wallensteen noted, conflict resolution is "ambitious as it tries to affect the basic issues, the incompatibilities that direct the conflicting parties."[16] Scholars and practitioners of conflict resolution grapple with the impact of global events and the ways in which changes in the international sphere impact decision-makers and the drivers of conflict. When successful, conflict resolution ends war non-violently and makes possible the beginning of longer-term work to change the relationship between warring parties (see "Conflict Transformation").

The term "conflict resolution" is also used outside of armed conflict to refer to the process by which two or more parties resolve a dispute with peaceful means. This process can take place between individuals, groups, or nations. While approaches to conflict resolution are multifaceted, common components include negotiation focused on common understanding and reasoning between parties, mediation whereby a third party helps disputants to reach an agreement, and arbitration whereby a neutral third party decides on the outcome of a dispute. In their 1991 book on negotiation, *Getting to Yes*, Fisher and Ury instruct disputants in the practice of using principled rather than hard or soft negotiation: they must be "soft on people and hard on the problem," proceed independent of trust, explore interests rather than positions, develop multiple options, use objective criteria, employ and be open to reason, and yield to principle and not pressure.[17]

16. Wallensteen, *Understanding Conflict Resolution*, 6.
17. Fisher and Ury, *Getting to Yes*, 13.

Suggested Reading

Fisher, Roger, and William Ury. *Getting to Yes: Negotiating Agreement Without Giving In*. Edited by Bruce Patton. New York: Penguin, 2011.

Shonk, Katie. "What Is Conflict Resolution, and How Does It Work?" *Daily Blog: Harvard Law School Program on Negotiation*, Dec. 25, 2024. https://www.pon.harvard.edu/daily/conflict-resolution/what-is-conflict-resolution-and-how-does-it-work/.

Wallensteen, Peter. *Understanding Conflict Resolution*. 6th ed. Los Angeles: Sage, 2023.

CONFLICT TRANSFORMATION

Conflict transformation is to envision and respond to the ebb and flow of social conflict as life-giving opportunities for creating constructive change processes that reduce violence, increase justice in direct interaction and social structures, and respond to real-life.

—JOHN PAUL LEDERACH

Whereas conflict resolution focuses on ending an ongoing conflict, conflict transformation views conflict as a potential catalyst for positive change. It aims to transform the relationships, systems, and structures that contributed to the conflict's occurrence. Peace scholar, John Paul Lederach, one of the foundational thinkers on conflict transformation, describes conflict transformation as a process and emphasizes the importance of taking a long-term view when addressing conflict.

Suggested Reading

Lederach, John Paul. *The Little Book of Conflict Transformation: Clear Articulation of the Guiding Principles by a Pioneer in the Field*. New York: Good Books, 2003.

COSMOPOLITANISM

I am not an Athenian or a Greek, but a citizen of the world.

—Socrates

When the cynic philosopher Diogenes—famous for living in a large ceramic jar and existing in intentional poverty among the ancient Greeks of Athens and Corinth—was asked where he came from, he replied that he was a *cosmopolite*—a citizen of the world. Cosmopolitanism, as a philosophy and political theory, embodies the belief that human beings, with all their individual differences, belong to a single community and have equal worth. Cosmopolitans place loyalty to humanity above loyalty to a specific group, believing that humans have a responsibility to one another as members of a global community. Albert Einstein, who changed nationalities multiple times throughout his life, rejected his German citizenship when the Nazi party came to power, and argued for one world government, wrote,

> A human being is part of a whole, called by us the "Universe," part limited in time and space. He experiences himself, his thoughts and feelings, as something separated from the rest—a kind of optical delusion of his consciousness. This delusion is a kind of prison for us, restricting us to our personal desires and to affection for a few persons nearest us. Our task must be to free ourselves from this prison by widening our circles of compassion to embrace all living creatures and the whole of nature in it beauty.[18]

Philosopher Martha Nussbaum, in her argument for placing cosmopolitanism above patriotism, said it thus:

> We should recognize humanity wherever it occurs, and give its fundamental ingredients, reason and moral capacity, our first allegiance and respect.... We should give our first allegiance to no mere form of government, no

18. Einstein, *Expanded Quotable Einstein*, 316.

temporal power, but to the moral community made up by the humanity of all human beings.[19]

Suggested Reading

Nussbaum, Martha C. *For Love of Country?* Boston: Beacon, 2002.
Van Hooft, Stan. *Cosmopolitanism: A Philosophy for Global Ethics.* London: Routledge, 2014. https://doi.org/10.4324/9781315711577.

CONSCIENTIOUS OBJECTION

Mankind must put an end to war, or war will put an end to mankind. . . . War will exist until that distant day when the conscientious objector enjoys the same reputation and prestige that the warrior does today.

—JOHN F. KENNEDY

Conscientious objection is a sincere conviction against bearing arms or participating in war. Mennonites in Europe first developed conscientious objection as a doctrine in the sixteenth century, followed by the Society of Friends (Quakers) in seventeenth-century England and by the Church of the Brethren and the Dukhobor religious sect in eighteenth-century Russia. Conscientious objectors might oppose serving in combat (taking part in noncombative military roles) or might oppose all types of military service. While conscientious objectors base their position on a range of religious, political, and philosophical views, they typically object to war in general, as opposed to a particular war, and represent thoughtfully constructed beliefs that have evolved over time. Several countries around the world have legislation exempting contentious objectors from forced conscription or providing alternatives such as military taxes or community service.

19. Nussbaum, *For Love*, 7.

Suggested Reading

Çaltekin, Demet Aslı. *Conscientious Objection in Turkey: A Socio-Legal Analysis of the Right to Refuse Military Service*. Edinburgh: Edinburgh University, 2022.

Matheson, John H. "Conscientious Objection to Military Service." *Free Speech Center at Middle Tennessee State University*. https://www.mtsu.edu/first-amendment/article/912/conscientious-objection-to-military-service/.

CRITICAL PEDAGOGY

Critical pedagogy (also referred to as liberatory pedagogy) is a philosophy of education described by one of its prolific spokespersons, Henry Giroux, as an "educational movement, guided by passion and principle, to help students develop consciousness of freedom, recognize authoritarian tendencies, and connect knowledge to power and the ability to take constructive action."[20] Critical pedagogy was first theorized by Brazilian educator, Paolo Frieire, in his 1970 publication *Pedagogy of the Oppressed*. Frieire described critical pedagogy as a pedagogy forged *with*, not *for*, the oppressed "in the incessant struggle to regain their humanity."[21] Frieire believed that through this approach to education, oppressed individuals and peoples would reflect on the causes of their oppression and engage in a struggle for liberation. Proponents of critical pedagogy are particularly attuned to relationships between teaching and learning and to the ways in which oppressive structures contribute to social injustice. They seek to develop in students an awareness of the systems and narratives that underpin oppression—what Freire calls *conscientization*—and to transform this awareness into action through the expression of human agency—what Freire refers to as *praxis*.

Suggested Reading

Darder, Antonia, et al. *International Critical Pedagogy Reader*. New York: Routledge, 2016.

20. Giroux, "Lessons from Paula Freire."
21. Freire, *Pedagogy of the Oppressed*, 48.

Freire, Paulo. *Pedagogy of the Oppressed*. 30th anniversary ed. New York: Continuum, 2000.

CULTURE OF PEACE

In 1988, the UN General Assembly adopted resolution A/RES/52/13 calling "for the promotion of a culture of peace" based on principles established in the UN Charter and on "respect for human rights, democracy and tolerance, the promotion of development, education for peace, the free flow of information and the wider participation of women as an integral approach to preventing violence and conflicts, and efforts aimed at the creation of conditions for peace and its consolidation."[22] The following year, UN resolution A/RES/53/243 outlined a program of action for the achievement of such a culture. Article 1 of the resolution defined a culture of peace as "a set of values, attitudes, traditions and modes of behaviour and ways of life"[23] based on the following principles and fostered by a national and international environment conducive to peace:

a. respect for life, ending of violence and promotion and practice of nonviolence through education, dialogue and cooperation;

b. full respect for the principles of sovereignty, territorial integrity and political independence of states and non-intervention in matters which are essentially within the domestic jurisdiction of any state, in accordance with the Charter of the UN and international law;

c. full respect for and promotion of all human rights and fundamental freedoms;

d. commitment to peaceful settlement of conflicts;

e. efforts to meet the developmental and environmental needs of present and future generations;

f. respect for and promotion of the right to development;

22. UN, A/RES/52/13.

23. UN, "Declaration and Programme."

g. respect for and promotion of equal rights and opportunities for women and men;

h. respect for and promotion of the right of everyone to freedom of expression, opinion and information;

i. and adherence to the principles of freedom, justice, democracy, tolerance, solidarity, cooperation, pluralism, cultural diversity, dialogue and understanding at all levels of society and among nations.[24]

While non-binding for member-states, the culture of peace resolutions recognized that peace is integrally connected with other issues of global concern, ranging from tolerance and discrimination to the recognition of full rights for peoples across the world. The resolutions also identified the role and responsibility of key institutions such as education, government, and civil society in advancing a culture of peace.

Suggested Reading

UN. "United Nations General Assembly, Resolution 52/13. Culture of Peace, A/RES/52/13 Jan 15, 1998." https://docs.un.org/en/A/RES/52/13.

DEPARTMENT OF PEACE

It is to be hoped that no objection will be made to the establishment of such an office . . . for as the *War-Office* of the United States was established in the *time of peace*, it is equally reasonable that a *Peace-Office* should be established in the *time of war*.

—BENJAMIN RUSH

A Department of Peace is a proposed, but not yet instituted, cabinet-level department of the US federal government committed to

24. See UN, A/RES/52/13. See also, Department of Peacebuilding Act, H.R. 1111, 118th Cong. (2023).

broad-scale investment in peacebuilding. The argument for a government entity devoted to peace goes back to 1798, when Benjamin Rush proposed that a peace-office be created to promote and preserve perpetual peace in the US. Rush—a medical doctor and signatory to the US Constitution—wrote as the newly established nation fought with indigenous peoples of North America over land and resources. A Christian, anti-slavery activist, and believer in the universal and equal liberty of all peoples, Rush advocated for a Secretary of Peace who would be perfectly free from the "absurd and vulgar" prejudices that shaped the practice of governance.[25] A Department of Peace—a modern iteration of Rush's idea—was proposed by Carrie Chapman Catt, founder of the League of Women Voters, in 1925. Since then, more than twenty legislators have proposed bills that would institute a Department of Peace within the US federal government. Noting the high economic cost of conflict, military spending, and responses to domestic cases of violence, proponents of a Department of Peace argue for a reallocation of federal monies currently spent on violence-reducing initiatives to peacebuilding, development, and humanitarian aid. While proposals have differed in specifics over the past century, common components have included the creation of a Secretary of Peace and the establishment of a Peace Academy (modeled after military academies), which would provide four years of education and training in exchange for five years of work in public service programs dedicated to national or international nonviolent conflict resolution. Advocates for a Department of Peace see it as a needed parallel institution to the US Department of War (now the US Department of Defense) and argue for a paradigm shift in which strategic peacebuilding is viewed as integral to the creation of national and global security.

Suggested Reading

Rush, Benjamin. "Essays, Literary, Moral, and Philosophical by Benjamin Rush, M.D. and Professor of the Institutes of Medicine and Clinical Practice

25. Rush, "Essays."

in the University of Pennsylvania." In the digital collection Evans Early American Imprint Collection. University of Michigan Library Digital Collections. https://name.umdl.umich.edu/N25938.0001.001.

Department of Peacebuilding Act of 2023, H.R. 1111. 118th Cong. (2023). https://www.congress.gov/bill/118th-congress/house-bill/1111/text#toc-HB751F7F2086448ADBB7AFB80631D4C89.

DISARMAMENT

You cannot simultaneously prevent and prepare for war.

—ALBERT EINSTEIN

"Disarmament" is a term often associated with "arms control" but connoting the complete elimination or strict control of various kinds of weapons. Proponents of disarmament do not deny the practical challenges and risks of disarming heavily armed societies—as David Barash and Charles Webel wrote, "The possession of weaponry is like riding a tiger: not only dangerous, it requires great care in extricating oneself!"[26] Still, advocates maintain that the reduction of weapons in our world—and especially of weapons capable of ending our world—holds incalculable value for the future of mankind and our planet. Approaches to disarmament include the following:

1. General and Complete Disarmament (GCD)—the complete elimination of weapons from all countries.

2. Maintenance of National Security Capabilities, articulated in Woodrow Wilson's Fourteen Points as national disarmament "to the lowest point consistent with domestic safety."[27]

3. Selective (or Qualitative) Disarmament—the elimination of offensive but not defensive weapons.

4. Weapons of Mass Destruction—mutually agreed disarmament of nuclear, atomic, biological, and chemical weapons.

26. Barash and Webel, *Peace and Conflict Studies*, 265.
27. National WWI Museum and Memorial, "Fourteen Points."

5. Weapons-Free Zones—agreements to eliminate all or certain types of weapons (such as nuclear) from a designated geographic area.

Suggested Reading

Barash, David P., and Charles Webel. *Peace and Conflict Studies*. 5th ed. Thousand Oaks, CA: Sage, 2021.
UN Office of Disarmament Affairs. "Treaty on the Non-Proliferation of Nuclear Weapons (NPT)." https://www.un.org/disarmament/wmd/nuclear/npt/.

ECONOMIC JUSTICE

Economic justice is a component of social justice dedicated to building economic institutions around principles of equal opportunity and distribution. The goal of economic justice is to create an economy in which every individual has the chance to establish a sufficient material foundation for a dignified and productive life, contributing to a more successful and just economic and social order and allowing individuals to engage beyond economics in the creative work of the mind and spirit.

Suggested Reading

Center for Economic and Social Justice. https://www.cesj.org.
Pogge, Thomas W. *World Poverty and Human Rights*. 2nd ed. Cambridge: Polity Press, 2008.

ENVIRONMENTAL ETHICS

When we see land as a community to which we belong, we may begin to use it with love and respect.

—ALDO LEOPOLD

In its widest sense, environmental ethics includes the natural environment of the earth and its ecosystems from the perspective of ethics, which raises questions of concern about value and obligation, questions about how we should regard the environment, the sort of value we should attach to it, and the moral obligations that we have towards it. Many of these questions have held deep significance for indigenous peoples around the world. Sometime in the mid-1800s, Seathl, chief of the Suquamish Native American peoples, wrote, "The earth does not belong to man, man belongs to the earth. All things are connected like the blood that unites us all. Man did not weave the web of life, he is merely a strand in it. Whatever he does to the web, he does to himself."[28]

Environmental ethics also grew out of the teachings of the German philosopher Immanuel Kant. But it has undergone much rethinking in the last fifty years as science has helped us see that the earth and its ecosystems is a living whole worthy of moral respect. It includes the human world as a part that depends on the well-being of the whole. But it is a fragile system, and one which science has also shown to be seriously threatened by the mindless use of human technologies in the realms of transportation, mining, agriculture, defense, and extravagant use of scarce resources. The fragility of the ecosystems was brought home powerfully by marine biologist Rachael Carson in her 1962 bestseller *Silent Spring*, which exposed the dangers of chemicals to the ecosystem and led the US Congress to ban the pesticide DDT a few years later. It could be said that environmental ethics became part of the curricula of higher education and more generally a part of public awareness partly because of her book. One of the lessons that has come with the new interest in environmental ethics is a new awareness of the value of our earth and our moral obligation—individually and collectively—of stewardship toward it.

Environmental ethics has also been adopted as a platform for "Green" political movements. The Green political ideology (and party) sprang up in Germany in the late 1970s with the primary aim of creating an ecologically sustainable planet. Today, Green

28. Seathl, "Chief Seattle's Letter."

parties are active in many of the world's countries. In their quest for environmental sustainability, which they see as an essential component of social justice, these movements place value on nonviolence, democracy, and civil liberties. The four pillars of the Green Party are ecological wisdom, social justice, grassroots democracy, and nonviolence.

Suggested Reading

Reardon, Betty. *Learning Peace: The Promise of Ecological and Cooperative Education.* Albany: SUNY, 1994.

GENEVA CONVENTIONS

A series of international treaties concluded in Geneva, Switzerland, between 1864 and 1949, the Geneva Conventions established rules for the humanitarian treatment of noncombatants (civilians, aid workers, and medics) and soldiers who can no longer participate in combat (prisoners of war, sick, wounded, or shipwrecked troops). In 1977, two protocols were added to the conventions that enabled fact-finding commissions for potential breaches of the convention, extended the conventions' protection to peoples in wars of self-determination, and articulated specific human rights protections for persons involved in violent civil conflicts, such as protection from torture, slavery, rape, terrorism, and the taking of hostages. The Geneva Conventions were applied to maritime warfare through the 1899 and 1907 Hague Conventions and have since become a bedrock of international law. The principles laid forth in the Geneva Conventions have been incorporated into international war crimes tribunals as well as the 1998 Rome Statute, which created the International Criminal Court.

Suggested Reading

Bothe, Michael, et al. *New Rules for Victims of Armed Conflicts: Commentary on the Two 1977 Protocols Additional to the Geneva Conventions of 1949.* 2nd ed. Leiden: Brill, 2013. https://doi.org/10.1163/9789004254718.

International Committee of the Red Cross. "The Geneva Conventions and Their Commentaries." https://www.icrc.org/en/document/geneva-conventions-1949-additional-protocols.

HAGUE CONVENTIONS

Held in 1899 at the invitation of Russian minister of foreign affairs Count Mikhail Nikolayevich Muravyov, and again in 1907, the Hague Conventions were early efforts to establish mutual international agreements on the limitation of armaments, the prohibition of weaponry such as asphyxiating gases and expanding bullets, the treatment of prisoners and wounded, humanitarian protections for noncombatants, and arbitration procedures for the settlement of disputes. The conventions were attended by twenty-six and forty-four states respectively. While the conferences failed to achieve their initial goal of limiting the armaments of states, they resulted in several international agreements—including the Convention for the Pacific Settlement of International Disputes—and the establishment of a permanent court of arbitration. The Hague Conventions demonstrated that the world's nations could arrive at solutions through dialogue. Although a third planned-for meeting in 1915 failed to materialize because of the outbreak of World War I, the conventions provided a rough prototype for the League of Nations, created at the end of the war.

Suggested Reading

Banks, William C. *New Battlefields, Old Laws: Critical Debates on Asymmetric Warfare.* New York: Columbia University Press, 2011. https://www.degruyter.com/isbn/9780231526562.

Schindler, Dietrich, and Jiří. Toman. *The Laws of Armed Conflicts: A Collection of Conventions, Resolutions, and Other Documents.* 4th rev. and completed ed. Leiden: Brill, 2004. http://site.ebrary.com/id/10175395.

GLOBAL ZERO

Global Zero was a global campaign launched in 2008 by more than three hundred international leaders with the goal of eliminating nuclear weapons. The initial campaign proposed a four-stage process by which the world could eliminate nuclear weapons by 2030:

1. 2010–2013: a bilateral treaty between Russia and the US to reduce total nuclear weapons to one thousand.

2. 2014–2018: a multilateral agreement whereby the US and Russia reduce to five hundred total weapons provided other nuclear nations freeze their stockpiles and establish a system for enforcement and verification.

3. 2019–2023: negotiate a treaty among all nuclear-capable nations to eliminate nuclear weapons in phased, verifiable steps by 2030.

4. 2024–2030: complete the agreed reductions and continue verification and enforcement.[29]

When Global Zero presented its plan, it pointed out that in the previous twenty years Russia and the US had together already destroyed some forty thousand nuclear weapons—twice as many as the twenty-year Global Zero plan would need to eliminate to achieve a world free of nuclear weapons.

Suggested Reading

Global Zero. https://www.globalzero.org/.

HAGUE APPEAL FOR PEACE

The Hague Appeal for Peace is a global network of people and organizations dedicated to the abolition of war and the securement of peace as a human right. At a 1999 conference celebrating the centennial of the first Hague Peace Conference, which

29. Global Zero, "Road Map."

resulted in the 1899 Hague Convention, the Hague Appeal for Peace launched the Global Campaign for Peace Education. The campaign developed stories from around the world that could be adapted to any culture in the service of promoting values and skills that contribute to a culture of peace. A 2015 publication based on the "Hague Agenda for Peace and Justice for the 21st Century" (UN Ref.A/54/98), *Peace Lessons from Around the World*, included stories from Albania, Cambodia, Philippines, Kenya, India, Nepal, the US, Catalunya (Spain), and South Africa. In 2006, the work of the Hague Appeal for Peace transitioned to Peace Boat US—a New York based organization that, in partnership with the non-governmental organization Peace Boat based in Japan, promotes opportunities for cross-cultural learning, advocacy, and cooperation.

Suggested Reading

Global Campaign for Peace Education. "Peace Lessons from Around the World." https://www.peace-ed-campaign.org/?s=peace+lessons+from+around+the+world.

Peace Boat US. http://www.peaceboat-us.org.

Sandy, Leo. "Creating a Culture of Peace: Notes from the Hague Appeal for Peace." *TESOL Matters* (1999). http://jupiter.plymouth.edu/~lsandy/hague.html.

INTERNATIONAL COURT OF JUSTICE

The International Court of Justice (ICJ) is the main judicial tribunal of the UN, to which all member states are parties. Informally referred to as the World Court, the ICJ was established by the UN in 1946. It replaced the former Permanent Court of International Justice, which had operated within The Hague, Netherlands, since 1922. Like its predecessor, the headquarters of the ICJ is in the Peace Palace at The Hague. The function of the ICJ is to resolve disputes between sovereign states. The court is comprised of fifteen elected jurists from different countries.

Suggested Reading

International Court of Justice. https://www.icj-cij.org/en/court.

INTERNATIONAL CRIMINAL COURT

The International Criminal Court (ICC) was established by the international treaty known as the Rome Statute and came into effect in 2002. To date, 124 nations are parties to the Rome Statute. Located in The Hague, the ICC prosecutes individuals indicted for genocide, war crimes, crimes against humanity, and international aggression. The ICC is set up to be a court of last resort, trying individuals when states are unable or unwilling to do so. The court can open cases in three ways: when a state party refers a situation in another country or in its own (as Ugandan president Yoweri Museveni did in 2004) through a referral from the UN Security Council, or on the initiative of the ICC Prosecutor.

The ICC has been challenged by limited enforcement mechanisms. It does not have its own police force but relies on UN member states to arrest individuals for whom warrants have been issued. In 2024, the ICC had thirty outstanding arrest warrants. Some prominent states have not joined the ICC, including China, India, Israel, Russia, and the US. Russia and Israel refused to recognize arrest warrants issued by the ICC in 2024 for their respective heads of state and high-level politicians. The US has supported the indictment and trial of other countries' citizens but objects to the possibility of its own nationals being tried by the ICC.

Despite these challenges, the creation of the court marked an evolution in international law. In 2006, Thomas Lubanga from the Democratic Republic of Congo became the first person arrested under authority of the ICC for war crimes (including conscripting child soldiers). He was sentenced in 2012 to fourteen years imprisonment.

Suggested Reading

International Criminal Court. https://www.icc-cpi.int/.

INTERNATIONAL LAW

Coined by the English philosopher Jeremy Bentham (1748–1832), the term "international law" refers to the body of laws and customs that govern the conduct and relations of sovereign states as well as the relations between states, international organizations, and individuals. Although we tend to think of international law as mainly concerned with issues of war and peace, it encompasses many spheres of global interaction, including trade, the environment, finance, management of marine resources, and human rights generally.

The idea of international law is as old as the nation-state itself. In 1625 the Dutch jurist Hugo Grotius published *On the Law of War and Peace*, which set forth the notion of a universal standard, or natural law, that exists above the law of nations, is discoverable by reason, and applies not merely to individuals in civil society but to nations and their interactions as well. Grotius believed that international law should promote the interests of peace through negotiated agreements and rules to avoid hostilities between sovereign states. A century and a half later, the German philosopher Immanuel Kant developed these ideas in his 1795 work *Perpetual Peace*. While Grotius believed that war, while undesirable, might sometimes be necessary to prevent international anarchy, Kant held that no war was ever just, and that it was the paramount moral business of the statesman to work to prevent hostilities and create lasting peace and security. Believing that republics were more conducive to international peace than monarchies and that standing state armies should be dismantled to discourage aggression, Kant envisioned international law advanced through a federation of free sovereign states.

Although the concept of international law as the safeguard of international peace is old, the codification of international laws concerning war and peace emerged at the turn of the twentieth century with the 1889 and 1907 Hague Conventions. While the idea of "laws of war" strikes some as an oxymoron, nearly all nations have recognized such laws as necessary to the security interests of all. This does not, of course, guarantee adherence to those laws (any more than it does with respect to domestic law). A sizable body of international law relating to war and peace exists today, covering the conditions under which war can be legally waged (see "Just War"), the conduct of states and individuals engaged in war (see "Geneva Conventions" and "Hague Conventions"), and mechanisms of arbitration and punishment for violations (see "International Court of Justice" and "International Criminal Court"). States confer on issues of international law through the UN.

Suggested Reading

UN. "Uphold International Law." https://www.un.org/en/our-work/uphold-international-law#:~:text=International%20law%20defines%20the%20legal,of%20individuals%20within%20State%20boundaries.

I-THOU RELATIONSHIP

Through the Thou a person becomes I.

—MARTIN BUBER

This is a philosophy centered on the ability of humans to engage with one another as whole beings through dialogue modeled on the relationship between God and human beings. The concept was introduced by the religious philosopher Martin Buber in his 1923 work, *I and Thou*. Buber believed that human existence could be defined by the way we engage in dialogue with God, with the world, and with each other. Too often, he argued, people engage with the specific, isolated qualities of a person, turning the encounter into one of "subject-object" (I-It) and leading to separation and detachment. Through dialogue modeled after the purest form of I-Thou relations (that between God and humankind), Buber believed people could experience relationships "subject-subject" (I-Thou*)*, leading to mutual caring, commitment, and responsibility. In such encounters, each participant can see the unity that they share as beings and can enter into the reality of the other. He saw "I-Thou" interactions between people as necessary for the productive resolution of conflict. In Buber's words,

> That peoples can no longer carry on authentic dialogue with one another is not only the most acute symptom of the pathology of our time, it is also that which most urgently makes a demand of us. I believe, despite all, that the peoples in this hour can enter into dialogue with one another. In a genuine dialogue each of the partners, even when he stands in opposition to the other, heeds, affirms, and confirms his opponent as an existing other. Only so can conflict certainly not be eliminated from the world, but be humanely arbitrated and led towards its overcoming.[30]

Suggested Reading

Buber, Martin. *I and Thou.* Translated by Ronald Gregor Smith. New York: Scribner's Sons, 1958.

JUST PEACE

A peace is of the nature of a conquest; for then both parties nobly are subdued, and neither party loser.

—WILLIAM SHAKESPEARE

Although the notion of a just peace might seem redundant (isn't peace "just" by definition?), it is one of the necessary conditions for a just war as spelled out in just war theory. If a war is to count as just it must (among other things) conclude in a just peace—that is,

---

30. Buber, *Pointing the Way*, 238.

a peace that meets the interests of justice. Just peace must include certain features. For example, it must seek to rectify the violations of rights that caused the war in the first place and should seek to hold accountable all those who violated the laws of war during the fighting. Just peace should vindicate justice without resorting to vindictiveness or victor's justice. It should also aid in the reconstruction of damaged property and people.

Suggested Reading

Allan, Pierre, and Alexis Keller, eds. *What Is a Just Peace?* Oxford: Oxford University Press, 2008.

JUST WAR DOCTRINE

This sounds like an oxymoron. Can war with its enormous suffering and killing really be just? Yes, according to the doctrine of just war. Just war doctrine goes back at least as far as the Roman philosopher Cicero in the first century BCE, but its development and importance to Christianity owes much to St. Augustine in the fifth century CE and St. Thomas Aquinas in the thirteenth century. Most early Christians were pacifists in accordance with the teachings of Jesus's teachings. When Christianity became the official state religion of the Roman Empire in the late fourth century CE, however, the leaders of the church felt obliged to reconcile the perceived need to protect the state from its enemies with the nonviolence of Christ's teachings. This was done largely with St. Augustine's help by means of just war theory, which attempted to identify the conditions required for waging a just war. The conditions—*all* of which must be met for a war to be considered just— are divided into two categories: conditions for going to war (*jus ad bellum*); and conditions for how war is conducted (*jus in bello*). The five conditions of *jus ad bellum* are:

1. Last Resort—war must be the last reasonable option after alternatives such as dialogue, diplomacy, and nonviolent political pressure have been exhausted.

2. Legitimate Authority—war must be declared by a sovereign authority.

3. Right Intention/Just Cause—war cannot be waged for vengeance, out of aggression, or for personal gain. The reason for waging war must be consistent with Christian principles or for the purposes of protecting civilians.

4. Reasonable Chance of Success—there must be a reasonable chance that war can successfully restore a just peace.

5. Goals of Peace/Proportionality—the goal of war must be the establishment of a just peace, and, recognizing that war is an inherent evil that causes great harm, war must prevent more suffering than it is expected to cause.[31]

The conditions for conducting war in a just way (*jus in bello*) include:

1. Military actions must conform to the principles of necessity and proportionality. Destruction must not exceed what is required for military success, and the harm caused must not outweigh the presumed benefits of the action (in other words, wide-scale bombing in order to achieve meager military progress would not be just, nor would the destruction of a city to neutralize a single munitions factory).

2. Military actions must conform to the principle of discrimination (or noncombatant immunity), which holds that civilians must not be the direct or intentional object of military action.[32]

While just war doctrine is frequently violated in modern warfare, many of its principles have been incorporated into international law and endorsed by most of the world's nations. Although it is

---

31. Barash and Webel, *Peace and Conflict Studies*, 441–44.
32. Barash and Webel, *Peace and Conflict Studies*, 441–44.

likely to remain aspirational in its vision of a war that is initiated and conducted in perfect accordance with its principles, just war doctrine's continued relevance in global norms around the proper waging of war demonstrates its lasting influence on how the world thinks about the ethics of war.

Suggested Reading

Carter, Joe. "A Brief Introduction to the Just War Tradition: *Jus ad Bellum*." The Ethics and Religious Liberty Commission of the Southern Baptist Convention, Aug. 17, 2017. https://erlc.com/resource/a-brief-introduction-to-the-just-war-tradition-jus-ad-bellum/.

KHAN'S PATHANS (KHUDAI KHIDMATGARS)

The Khudai Khidmatgar, or Servants of God, was a nonviolent resistance movement led by Khan Abdul Ghaffar Khan against British rule in India in the 1920s and 1930s. Based in northwest India, the Khudai Khidmatgar movement aimed to removed British rule through nonviolent action, education, the reformation of Pashtun society, and women's emancipation. At its height, the movement included over one hundred thousand members. Ghaffar Khan's Pashtuns (also called Pathans), who had a reputation for being among India's fiercest warriors, transformed into nonviolent soldiers ready to die for India. Every Pathan took an oath in which they promised to refrain from violence and revenge, to forgive those who oppressed them, and to live a life devoted to simplicity, virtue, and social work. Ghaffar Khan formed an alliance with Gandhi in the 1930s, and his Pathans became a significant force during the Indian National Congress's civil disobedience campaign. Gandhi was impressed by the Pathan's self-discipline and ability to resist responding with violence when provoked. Ghaffar Khan's Pathans withstood the brutal assault of the British and paved the way for more nonviolent skirmishes that ultimately caused the British to cede their colonial hold on India. As Robert Holmes and Barry Gan note, "The story of Khan's movement among the Pathans demonstrates the power of nonviolence to harness the negative forces in personality and use those same forces to transform an individual, a community, or even a society."[33]

Suggested Reading

Bakshi, S. R. "Role of Pathans in Civil Disobedience Movement 1930–34." *Proceedings of the Indian History Congress* 42 (1981) 473–81.

Holmes, Robert L., and Barry L. Gan. *Nonviolence in Theory and Practice*. 3rd ed. Belmont, CA: Wadsworth, 2011.

LEAGUE OF NATIONS

The League of Nations was an organization for international cooperation agreed to during the 1919 Paris Peace Conference and established on January 10, 1920 by the victorious Allied powers after World War I. The central idea behind the League of Nations was to create a body capable of preventing the crime of aggressive war through collective security. Members of the League pledged to aid fellow member states against an aggressive state through economic sanctions and, if necessary, military intervention. They also agreed to reduce their armaments, to respect each other's integrity and independence, and to submit serious disputes to the arbitration of a permanent international court (outlined by articles 13–15). In its early history, the League successfully settled disputes between Great Britain and Turkey and between Greece and Bulgaria. But as international law scholar Phillippe Sands noted, "This was a world of sovereign freedom, with few international rules to constrain the behavior of governments."[34] In the early 1930s the League proved ineffective in dealing with the aggressive actions of Italy, Japan, and Germany. When Hitler invaded Poland in 1939, France and England declared war against Germany without consulting the League. While the League failed to be the preventative mechanisms its founders had envisioned, its creation introduced into

33. Holmes, *Nonviolence in Theory*, 188.
34. Sands, *Lawless World*, 25.

international relations the concept of collective security as a means of stopping interstate war. The League was disbanded on April 19, 1946; its mandate was transferred to the newly created UN.

Suggested Reading

Gram-Skjoldager, Karen, and Haakon A. Ikonomou, eds. *The League of Nations: Perspectives from the Present*. Aarhus: Aarhus University Press, 2019.

LIBERATION THEOLOGY

When I give food to the poor, they call me a saint. When I ask why the poor have no food, they call me a Communist.

—ARCHBISHOP HÉLDER CÂMARA

The liberation theology movement arose from within the Roman Catholic Church in the twentieth century and gained its momentum in Latin America. The movement's founding document, composed at the 1968 Latin American Bishop's Conference in Medellín, Colombia, championed the rights of the poor and condemned industrialized countries for enriching themselves through the impoverishment of developing nations. Gustavo Gutiérrez, a Peruvian priest, wrote the movement's seminal text—*A Theology of Liberation*—in 1971. Early liberation theologians believed the Roman Catholic Church in Latin America should be directly involved in improving the lives of the poor and challenging oppressive socioeconomic structures. They believed that God speaks through the poor and that the Bible can only be properly understood from the poor's perspective. They saw the Bible as a call to action and believed its ideals could not be achieved through passive acquiescence in the face of social and economic injustice. The movement did its work through small groups of Christians living in community. These *communidades de base* (base communities) focused on the study of Scripture and the provision of practical needs such as food, water, shelter, and hygienic sewage disposal.

Opponents of liberation theology have criticized it for replacing a focus on the soul with a focus on the body, and some critics have accused the movement of advocating for a Marxist view of society. Despite these criticisms, tenets of Liberation Theology have been influential on the development of Catholic social teaching in the twenty-first century.

Suggested Reading

Zegarra, Raúl E. *A Revolutionary Faith: Liberation Theology Between Public Religion and Public Reason*. Standard: Stanford University, 2003.

LIMITED TEST BAN TREATY:1963

This treaty is among the first nuclear agreements of the Cold War. It prohibits testing of nuclear weapons in the atmosphere, outer space, and under water. It proclaims its principle aim to be "complete disarmament" and puts the nuclear parties (US, UK, and Soviet Union) on record as seeking a total test ban and agreeing to continue negotiations to this end.

Negotiations to limit testing began in the late 1950s due mainly to global concern over the growing dangers of radioactive fallout from testing in the atmosphere. Progress was slowed by general mistrust and concerns about verification. At one point, success was blocked by disagreement on the number of annual inspections—the Soviet Union agreed to three, the US insisted on six. But in October of 1962 the Cuban Missile Crisis brought the world to the edge of nuclear catastrophe and the superpowers to their cooperative senses; the partial test ban was concluded within a few months.

Nonetheless, it became clear that nuclear testing had only been driven underground—less dangerous to human health but suitable for testing new, lighter weapons. The nuclear arms race continued to accelerate. The roughly five hundred atmospheric tests were merely replaced by more than fifteen hundred underground tests until the end of the Cold War in 1991. A 1991 study by the International Physicians for the Prevention of Nuclear War found that continuing fallout from pre-1964 atmospheric testing would cause 430,000 cancer deaths worldwide by 2000.[35]

A total test ban guaranteed by treaty is still needed globally. In 1996 the Comprehensive Test Ban Treaty (CTBT) was approved by the UN General Assembly for international signatures and ratification. But as of 2024, eight states out of the forty-four listed as having nuclear capabilities—China, Egypt, India, Iran, Israel, North Korea, Pakistan, and the US—must ratify the treaty for it to come into force.

Suggested Reading

Krepon, Michael. *Winning and Losing the Nuclear Peace: The Rise, Demise, and Revival of Arms Control.* Stanford: Stanford University, 2021.

MCCLOY–ZORIN AGREEMENT

This 1961 agreement concerning US–Soviet disarmament was named for the respective American and Soviet negotiators. It wasn't an agreement to disarm; rather, it was an agreement concerning the procedures and principles that any future disarmament treaty must conform to. Among its requirements it included the following:

1. general and complete disarmament and reliable procedures for settling disputes nonviolently

2. the retention of non-nuclear armed forces solely for domestic order and UN peace forces

3. the end of military bases, stockpiles, and weapons

4. the creation of a disarmament organization and inspectors with unrestrained access

5. the creation of a UN peace force strong enough to deter or suppress violations of the UN Charter[36]

35. IPPNW, "Radioactive Heaven and Earth," 163.
36. Ratical.org, "McCloy/Zorin Agreement," 1–2.

While the Cold War precluded the possibility of such a treaty, it is nonetheless remarkable that both sides could agree on what a genuine disarmament must include. Two years later, the US and Soviet Union agreed to the 1963 Limited Test Ban Treaty.

Suggested Reading

Ratical.org. "The McCloy/Zorin Agreement." https://ratical.org/ratville/JFK/HWNAU/MZappIX.pdf.

NEW THINKING

"New thinking" is a term associated with Mikhail Gorbachev's re-forms of the Soviet Union in the years leading up to the end of the Cold War (1985–1991). Influenced by the 1955 "Russell–Einstein Manifesto," Gorbachev's new thinking was based on the twin ideas of international cooperation and common security, according to which genuine security could only be mutual and could not be gained at the expense of the other side's interest. In keeping with the new thinking, Gorbachev met US president Ronald Reagan at Rejkyavik in 1986 and came very close to an agreement to elimi-nate all nuclear weapons. But they couldn't agree to deploy a Star Wars missile defense system that Reagan made as a condition for nuclear disarmament (missile defenses were then outlawed by the ABM Treaty and Gorbachev saw them as potentially offensive). But the very next year they did conclude the Intermediate-range Nuclear Forces (INF) Treaty by which all such US and Soviet mis-siles (some 2,700) in Europe and the Soviet Union were destroyed. To hasten an agreement on NATO and Warsaw Pact conventional weapons in Europe, Gorbachev began a series of unilateral with-drawals that soon led to the 1990 Treaty on Conventional Armed Forces in Europe. At the same time, important progress was being made in the Strategic Arms Reduction Talks (START). This led to the START I Treaty in 1991 by which the superpowers reduced their long-range (strategic) nuclear weapons by 50 percent Since then, continued START agreements have reduced the deployed strategic US-Russia weapons to about 12 percent of what they were when Gorbachev came on the international scene in the mid-1980s.[37]

Domestically, Gorbachev's new thinking was associated with the terms *perestroika* (roughly translated as "rebuilding") and *glasnost* ("openness"). These were the watchwords of his liberal reforms that included decentralization of the economy, increased freedom of speech, and reduced censorship.

Suggested Reading

Einstein, Albert, et al. "The Russell–Einstein Manifesto." International Peace Movement. https://scarc.library.oregonstate.edu/coll/pauling/peace/papers/peace6.007.5.html.

US Department of State Archive. "Gorbachev and New Thinking in Soviet Foreign Policy, 1987–88." https://2001-2009.state.gov/r/pa/ho/time/rd/108225.htm.

NOBEL PEACE PRIZE

Swedish chemist and inventor Alfred Nobel established the Nobel Peace Prize through his 1895 will to honor "those, who, during the preceding year, shall have conferred the greatest benefit on mankind."[38] Nobel was actively engaged with social issues and the international peace movement. His acquaintance with Bertha von Suttner, who was a driving force in the peace movement in Europe and was later awarded the Peace Prize, influenced his views. The Nobel Prize offers categories in peace, literature, physics, chemistry, and medicine. The Nobel Peace Prize has been awarded to more than one hundred individuals and to organizations such as the International Committee of the Red Cross and the UN High Commissioner for Refugees. The Norwegian Parliament elects the committee that makes award selections.

---

37. US Department of State Archive, "Gorbachev and New Thinking."
38. Nobel Prize, "Man Behind the Prize."

Suggested Reading

The Nobel Prize. "The Nobel Peace Prize." https://www.nobelprize.org/prizes/peace/.

NON-GOVERNMENTAL ORGANIZATION (NGO)

We have to learn to think in a new way. We have to learn to ask ourselves, not what steps can be taken to give military victory to whatever group we prefer, for there no longer are such steps; the question we have to ask ourselves is: what steps can be taken to prevent a military contest of which the issue must be disastrous to all parties?

—Bertrand Russell and Albert Einstein

Although the term lacks a precise definition, NGOs are generally non-profit organizations unconnected with governments. While non-partisan in the narrow sense, they have broad sociopolitical objectives such as human rights, poverty, the environment, and war and peace. The concept was first introduced in 1945 by the UN, which allowed certain non-government groups observer status at some of its meetings.

NGOs are often seen as representatives of civil society that advocate for the citizen. They can, of course, reflect unduly narrow interests and the biases of their funding sources, causing consequences for local communities (for example, by undermining local leadership, creating aid dependency, or altering local economies). Yet many have unquestionably played a significant part in the quest for a more humane and peaceful world. Many NGOs have provided valuable contributions to international problems that need information and management. The role of the NGO was greatly enhanced by the end of the Cold War and the planetary interconnectedness fostered by globalization. Valuable contributions have been made, and continue to be made, by organizations such as the Red Cross, Greenpeace, Oxfam, Natural Resources Defense Council, Doctors without Borders, Physicians for Social Responsibility,

Veterans for Peace, Pugwash Conferences on Science and World Affairs, and Amnesty International, to name only a very few.

Suggested Reading

World Association of Non-Governmental Organizations. https://www.wango. org.

NON-PROVOCATIVE DEFENSE

Non-provocative defense is a strategy advocated for by the World BEYOND War movement and involves the demilitarization of security forces and the adoption of weapons systems used exclusively for defense. Non-provocative defense includes the elimination of offensive weapons such as intercontinental ballistic missiles, militarized drones, nuclear submarine fleets, aircraft carriers, and long-range attack aircraft. *A Global Security System: An Alternative to War*, now in its fifth edition, outlines the strategy in full and connects it to nonviolent conflict management and the creation of a culture of peace.

Suggested Reading

Shifferd, Kent D., et al. *A Global Security System: An Alternative to War.* 5th ed. Charlottesville, VA: World Beyond War, 2020. http://public.eblib.com/ choice/PublicFullRecord.aspx?p=6275620.

NONVIOLENT ACTION

Non-violence is the greatest force at the disposal of mankind. It is mightier than the mightiest weapon of destruction devised by the ingenuity of man.

—MAHATMA GANDHI

Nonviolent action, as theorized by the late scholar Gene Sharp, is based on the premise that rulers derive their power from the consent of their subjects and that subjects can withdraw that consent through strategic actions. Using the metaphor of pillars, Sharp argued that it was ultimately the cooperation and obedience of large numbers of people that support the state institutions on which rulers rely. "You take away the sources of power and the man who was formerly a tyrant becomes just an old man," he noted. Sharp identified 198 techniques of nonviolent action that he placed in the categories of symbolic protest, noncooperation, and intervention. The degree of risk increases as one moves from symbolic protest to intervention. For example, under protest are marches and vigils; under noncooperation are boycotts, strikes, and nonpayment of fees and rent; and under intervention are sit-ins, hunger strikes, civil disobedience, and nonviolent obstruction and occupation. Each action is intended to systematically remove consent from key institutions, or pillars, that allow society to function. As Eric Stoner aptly summarized,

> Some of these pillars, such as the military, the police and the courts, are coercive in nature, compelling obedience through force or the threat thereof, while other pillars, like the media, education system, and religious institutions, support the system through their influence over culture and popular opinion. Hence, the power of even the most charismatic or ruthless leader is contingent upon the support of key institutions, themselves vulnerable to popular action or withdrawal of consent from the general population.[39]

Sharp's theory of nonviolent action has been a catalyst for nonviolent resistance in many parts of the world. His 1993 handbook, *From Dictatorship to Democracy*, in which he gave a prescription for the overthrow of dictatorships, has been translated into thirty-one languages. His work has been noted as an inspiration by people who participated in the Arab Spring and in places like Burma, Ukraine, and Serbia; meanwhile, dictatorships in

---

39. Stoner, "Beautiful Trouble."

countries such as Iran and Venezuela have labeled Sharp an enemy of the state. The Albert Einstein Institute, a Boston-based non-profit founded by Sharp and devoted to studying and promoting the use of nonviolent action in conflicts, continues to explore the practical implementation of nonviolent action today.

Suggested Reading

Chenoweth, Erica, and Maria J. Sephan. *Why Civil Resistance Works: The Strategic Logic of Nonviolent Conflict.* New York: Columbia University Press, 2011.

Engler, Mark. "The Machiavelli of Nonviolence: Gene Sharp and the Battle Against Corporate Rule." *Dissent,* fall 2013. https://www.dissentmagazine.org/article/the-machiavelli-of-nonviolence-gene-sharp-and-the-battle-against-corporate-rule/.

NORWEGIAN RESISTANCE

Even though Norway's pacifist posture after World War I left it militarily unprepared to defend against the Nazi invasion of April 1940, the country organized a resistance movement that gave the occupiers serious problems. While part of the resistance involved military force through the agency of the Norwegian secret army (Milorg), much of it was consistent with nonviolent principles including non-cooperation and civil disobedience. One notable event was a strike by Norwegian teachers who refused to teach Nazi propaganda in their schools. One thousand teachers were sent to concentration camps; they were eventually released and received a hero's welcome back home. This example serves as one of many remarkable resistance movements worldwide.

Suggested Reading

Sharp, Gene. *Waging Nonviolent Struggle: Twentieth Century Practice and Twenty-First Century Potential.* Boston: Extending Horizons, 2005.

Skodvin, Magne. "Norwegian Non-Violent Resistance During the German Occupation." In *The Strategy of Civilian Defense: Nonviolent Resistance to*

Aggression, edited by Adam Roberts, 135–41. London: Faber and Faber, 1967.

NUCLEAR NONPROLIFERATION TREATY

The important 1968 Nuclear Nonproliferation Treaty (NPT) offered nuclear power technology to non-nuclear states in exchange for adherence to international controls on nuclear fuel and abstinence from building nuclear weapons, subject to international verification. In turn, the nuclear weapon states pledged to seek "cessation of the nuclear arms race at an early date" and a treaty on "general and complete disarmament under strict and effective international controls."[40]

Suggested Reading

Arms Control Association. "The Nuclear Proliferation Treaty (NPT) at a Glance." https://www.armscontrol.org/factsheets/nptfact.

PACIFISM

There are causes worth dying for, but none worth killing for.

—ALBERT CAMUS

Pacifism encompasses a range of beliefs about the use of violence. Universal or absolute pacifism holds that all killing and violence (in war or otherwise) is morally wrong. Pragmatic pacifism, as peace scholar David Cortright noted, "can be understood as a continuum of perspectives, beginning on the one hand with the rejection of military violence and extending across a range of options that allow for some limited use of forced under specific conditions."[41] Those who practice private pacifism accept some cases of violence when employed by a state but reject all personal violence. Others

40. Arms Control Association, "Nuclear Nonproliferation."
41. Cortright, *Peace*, 14.

believe that there are times when personal violence is acceptable but oppose violence in war.

Suggested Reading

Cortright, David. *Peace: A History of Movements and Ideas.* Cambridge: Cambridge University Press, 2008.

Lackey, Douglas P. *The Ethics of War and Peace.* Englewood Cliffs, NJ: Prentice Hall, 1989.

PARTNERSHIP SOCIETY

In sum, the struggle for our future is . . . the struggle between those who cling to patterns of domination and those working for a more equitable partnership world.

—RIANE EISLER

Riane Eisler coined the term "partnership society" to refer to societies that focus on cooperation, relationship building, communication, gender equality, and nonviolence. She contrasted partnership societies with "dominator" societies where authoritarianism, male dominance, violence, and dehumanization are prevalent. In her seminal work, *The Chalice and the Blade: Our History, Our Future*, Eisler argued that human societies throughout history have existed on a continuum of dominator and partnership systems, and that early partnership societies exhibited higher levels of peace and equity. While dominator systems divide the world into in-groups and out-groups, defining the "other" as an enemy to be destroyed, partnership systems support mutually respectful relations, view conflict as an opportunity for creative change, and focus on empowering as opposed to disempowering others. Eisler maintained that this continuum provides better insights into societal values and institutions than conventional social categories such as capitalist vs. communist or right vs. left., and that a return to the partnership system that guided most societies in early human history (pre-5000 BC) would advance peace and equity in families, societies, and global relations.

Suggested Reading

Bates, Jordan. "'Dominator' vs. 'Partnership' Cultures: A Profound Retelling of Human History." Jordan Bates, Jan. 14, 2015. https://jordanbates.life/dominator-vs-partnership/.

Eisler, Riane. *The Chalice and the Blade: Our History, Our Future.* San Francisco: HarperOne, 2011.

PEACE

Peace is not the absence of war; it is a virtue, a state of mind, a disposition for benevolence, confidence, justice.

—BENEDICT SPINOZA

As Barash and Webel note, "Peace is surprisingly difficult to define. Like happiness, harmony, justice, and freedom, it is something we often recognize by its absence."[42] The simple absence of violence is sometimes referred to as negative peace. Alternatively, positive peace refers to contexts and actions that prevent both physical and structural violence and that contribute to sustainable harmonious relationships. In the words of Betty Reardon,

> Peace as affirmation of life is probably the most powerful and dynamic notion of positive peace. . . . It calls for struggle against the endemic poverty that shortens life and lowers the quality of life for the majority of the earth's peoples; against the chronic hunger and famine that sap the strength and extinguish the lives of millions; against a conventional arms race that saps resources and promotes lethal conflict within and among nations throughout the world; and against the proliferation of nuclear weapons that threatens the life of Earth itself.[43]

42. Barash and Webel, *Peace and Conflict Studies*, 5.
43. Reardon, *Comprehensive Peace Education*, 30–31.

For Reardon, the three components that make up education for positive peace include environmental education (preserving the ecological system), development education (increasing material well-being), and human rights education (recognizing the dignity and worth of all human beings). Since structural violence produces oppression that inhibits human development, all efforts to minimize structural violence through nonviolent means constitute positive peace.

Suggested Reading

Royce, A. "A Definition of Peace." *Peace and Conflict: Journal of Peace Psychology* 10 (2009) 101–16.

PEACEBUILDING

Unlike peacekeeping, which aims to uphold peace agreements and prevent recurrence of violence through temporary and minimal use of force, peacebuilding involves the "deliberate, sustained activities that are required to build enduring security and sustainable peace."[44] It focuses on developing constructive relationships in society and politics that cross boundaries like ethnicity, class, and religion. Peacebuilding employs nonviolent strategies to resolve injustice and transform structural conditions that make conflict more likely. "Peacebuilding can include conflict prevention; conflict management; conflict resolution and transformation, and post-conflict reconciliation."[45]

Suggested Reading

Kroc Institute for International Peace Studies. "What Is Strategic Peacebuilding?" https://kroc.nd.edu/about-us/what-is-peace-studies/what-is-strategic-peacebuilding/.

44. Welch, *Real Peace*, 53.
45. Kroc Institute, "Strategic Peacebuilding."

PEACE EDUCATION

The most violent element in society is ignorance.

—Emma Goldman

For Reardon, a leader in peace education, the transformational imperative of peace education is "to promote the development of an authentic planetary consciousness that will enable us to function as global citizens and to transform the present human condition by changing the social structures and the patterns of thought that have created it."[46] Transformational, comprehensive peace education is not just *about* peace but *for* peace. It must go beyond lectures that provide content about peace and embody, instead, a pedagogical process that models peace and inspires students to become peace activists and advocates. Peace educators employ a pedagogy of discomfort, encouraging students to critically examine their own values and attitudes about themselves and the world in which they live. They expose students to people, places, and ideas that are uniquely different from their own, not only welcoming controversy but vigorously pursuing it to create cognitive dissonance that leads to cognitive restructuring. Peace education also involves actions that allow students to experience change agency, such as writing letters, signing petitions, participating in demonstrations, attending public hearings, and joining organizations that promote peace and social/environmental justice. Authentic peace education requires a process that Freire called "conscientization," where knowledge and experience function in a reciprocal relationship as they inform each other.[47]

Suggested Reading

Meyer R., and Leo Sandy. "Educating for Global Citizenship in the New Millennium." *International Journal of Diversity in Organizations, Communities, and Nations* 9 (2009) 59–64.

46. Reardon, *Comprehensive Peace Education*, x.
47. Freire, *Pedagogy of the Oppressed*, 35.

49

Sandy, Leo R., and Ray Perkins. "The Nature of Peace and Its Implications for Peace Education." *OJPCR: The Online Journal of Peace and Conflict Resolution* 4 (2002) 1–8.

PEACEKEEPING

The goal of peacekeeping is to "protect human lives with as little force as possible."[48] Peacekeeping is a short-term intervention rather than one that focuses on long-term transformation. It seeks to uphold peace agreements and ceasefires and prevent the recurrence of armed violence. The UN has played a strong peacekeeping role since its inception; in 2024 it had eleven active peacekeeping operations. Peacekeeping is most effective when it works in tandem with strategic peacebuilding and conflict transformation.

Suggested Reading

UN Peacekeeping. https://peacekeeping.un.org/en.

PEACEFUL SOCIETIES

A Native American grandfather talking to his young grandson tells the boy he has two wolves inside of him struggling with each other. The first is the wolf of peace, love and kindness. The other wolf is fear, greed and hatred. "Which wolf will win, grandfather?" asks the young boy. "Whichever one I feed," is the reply.

— "The Two Wolves," a Cherokee Tale

It is often presumed that humans are aggressive by nature, thereby making the institution of war perpetual. However, the existence of several cultures that eschew violence provides a counterargument to this presumption. Just because humans have the capacity for

48. Welch, *Real Peace*, 27.

violence does not mean they have to exercise it. Humans also appear to be wired for empathy (Rifkin, 2010). The extent to which either is expressed depends largely on cultural factors that present themselves through parenting and teaching practices as well as media influence. Researchers have identified Inuit cultures in the Canadian Arctic and hunter-gatherer societies in tropical or subtropical regions that appear to eschew all inter-group violence. These societies tend to be egalitarian with anti-violence value systems that encourage generosity and gentleness over behaviors such as quarrelling, anger, and fighting.[49] There are a handful of cultures that meet many of the criteria for cultures of peace. The existence of such cultures provides evidence of the power of environment to change human behavior and suppress more primitive parts of the human psyche that can be invoked by other competing experiences.

Suggested Reading

Fabbro, David. "Peaceful Societies: An Introduction." *Journal of Peace Research* 15 (1978) 67–83.
Rifkin, J. (2010). *The Empathic Civilization*. https://www.ted.com/talks/jeremy_rifkin_the_empathic_civilization

PEACEMAKING

Peacemaking is a process that seeks to achieve a sustainable peace through negotiation with all parties involved through "Track One" diplomacy—"officially sanctioned government negotiations and policy initiatives, and through . . . the work of civilians at all levels of society to reach new understandings of and find nonviolent ways to resolve conflicts."[50]

49. Hinde and Rotblat, *War No More*, 68.
50. Welch, *Real Peace*, 41–42.

Suggested Reading

Mac Ginty, Roger, and Anthony Wanis-St. John. *Contemporary Peacemaking: Peace Processes, Peacebuilding, and Conflict.* 3rd ed. London: Palgrave Macmillan, 2022.

POSITIVE PEACE

See "Peace."

PUGWASH CONFERENCE ON SCIENCE AND WORLD AFFAIRS

This is an organization founded in 1957 by Joseph Rotblat to educate world leaders concerning the dangers of nuclear weapons. The organization was named after Pugwash, Nova Scotia, where the first conference was held. An early objective was to bring together scientists—many of them Nobel laureates—from both sides of the Iron Curtain to emphasize the dangers of nuclear war and to influence national policy regarding the main principle of the Russell–Einstein Manifesto (1955): that nuclear weapons, and ultimately war, must be abolished if humankind is to survive long-term. Pugwash is credited with making possible a recognition of common ground between the US and the Soviet Union that led directly to arms control agreements during the Cold War.

Rotblat, a British nuclear scientist and peace educator for more than fifty years, received the Nobel Peace Prize in 1995. Rotblat worked on the Manhattan Project to build the atomic bomb. He was the only scientist to resign from the project on moral grounds once Germany had been defeated since he believed that the sole justification for the bomb was to develop it before the Germans did. The Pugwash Conference on Science and World Affairs continues to promote scientific dialogue and engagement around nuclear weapons and weapons of mass destruction.

Suggested Reading

Pugwash Conferences on Science and World Affairs. https://pugwash.org/.

ROSENSTRASSE PROTESTS

In 1943, as part of a "final roundup," the Gestapo arrested around 1,800 Jewish men in Berlin who were married to non-Jewish women. When their wives heard about the arrest of their husbands and their detention at the Jewish Community Center in the Rosenstrasse, they arrived on the scene to search for their husbands but were stopped by SS guards. The women returned the next day and demanded the release of their husbands. They shouted "We want our husbands back" and "Let our husbands go." The women remained there for several days, and their ranks exceeded one thousand despite threats to be arrested and machine gunned. In the interim, some of their husbands were part of a shipment of prisoners sent by train to Auschwitz. The persistent pressure of the women caused the Gestapo to release their husbands. The Nazis even stopped the train to let them off on orders of Propaganda Minister Joseph Goebbels. Thirty-five intermarried Jews who had already been sent to Auschwitz were also returned to Berlin but for some reason twenty-five were not released. Apparently, the Nazis did not want the bad publicity at home or abroad, and they were not well prepared to deal effectively with nonviolent action. This raises the question as to whether more systematic and frequent expressions of nonviolence could have had a greater impact on the Nazis whose reflexes were geared more for counterviolence.

Suggested Reading

Mertnoff, Ela. "The Rosenstrasse Protests: Women's Collective Action Against the Nazi Regime." *La ventana. Revista de estudios de Género* 6 (2021) 145–74.

RUSSELL–EINSTEIN MANIFESTO

There lies before us, if we choose, continual progress in happiness, knowledge, and wisdom. Shall we, instead, choose death, because we cannot forget our quarrels? We appeal, as human beings, to human beings: Remember your humanity, and forget the rest. If you can do so, the way lies open to a new Paradise; if you cannot, there lies before you the risk of universal death.

—RUSSELL–EINSTEIN MANIFESTO

This document, named after philosopher Bertrand Russell and scientist Albert Einstein, was drafted mainly by Russell and signed by Einstein and nine other scientists of international repute in 1955. The main idea was to bring together respected authorities from both sides of the Iron Curtain—communist and non-communist—to publicly acknowledge the grave danger of nuclear weapons and war, and to pressure world powers to move together towards the abolition of both. The document is credited with initiating a transnational movement that brought new thinking to the superpower nuclear arms race and, ultimately, an end to the Cold War.

Suggested Reading

"The Russell–Einstein Manifesto." https://scarc.library.oregonstate.edu/coll/pauling/peace/papers/peace6.007.5.html.

SATYAGRAHA

Satyagraha is literally holding on to Truth and it means, therefore, Truth-force.

—MAHATMA GANDHI

Gandhi combined the words truth (*satya*) with love and firmness (*agraha*) to form *satyagraha*, a nonviolent force born of love and adherence to truth. Gandhi saw *satyagraha* as a way of life and emphasized its ability to change the hearts of one's opponents through civil disobedience and noncooperation. *Satyagraha* required an absolute avoidance of violence in thought and deed. Gandhi insisted that "one who is free from hatred requires no sword."[51] A *satyagrahi*, or someone committed to the practice of *satyagraha*, was expected to strictly obey all societal laws except those that were unjust. Then and only then was civil disobedience justified.

Suggested Reading

Mahatma Gandhi. "What Is Satyagraha?" https://www.mkgandhi.org/faq/q17.htm.

SHANTI SENA

This is a peacekeeping strategy in which the force majority of a country's citizens are trained in civilian-based defense, forming a peace force that would make it impossible for an invader or internal usurper to govern if the nation were attacked. The strategy holds that massive nonviolent actions would shut down government and industry, making it impossible for an attacker to control people or institutions.

Suggested Reading

White, R. "Review of *Gandhi's Peace Army: The Shanti Sena and Unarmed Peace-keeping*, by Thomas Weber." *Contemporary South Asia* 7 (1998) 114–15.

SOCIAL JUSTICE

Equality of opportunity is not enough. Unless we create an environment where everyone is guaranteed some minimum capabilities through some guarantee of minimum income, education, and healthcare, we cannot say that we have fair competition. When

51. Gandhi, *Gandhi Reader*, 116.

some people have to run a 100 metre race with sandbags on their legs, the fact that no one is allowed to have a head start does not make the race fair. Equality of opportunity is absolutely necessary but not sufficient in building a genuinely fair and efficient society.

—HA-JOON CHANG

Social justice generally refers to a kind of justice within society that reflects the values of solidarity and equality. In such a society, human rights are highly valued and protected. Social justice is distinct from legal justice, although a society's system of laws, if it is fair and equitable, can support and promote social justice. Social justice is not a religious concept per se, but major world religions emphasize social justice through concepts like charity, kindness, and the dignity of human life. Many non-religious organizations are also concerned with social justice, and often the dependent connection between peace and justice is explicitly articulated. For example, the International Labor Organization's constitution states that "universal and lasting peace can be established only if it is based upon social justice."[52] Social justice includes a sustainable environment. It is inextricably bound up with human rights, especially (but not exclusively) with what are sometimes called socioeconomic rights—rights to health care, education, and employment. Indeed, one could say that the ultimate value of all human rights is the promotion of social justice.

Suggested Reading

Capeheart, Loretta, and Dragan Milovanovic. *Social Justice: Theories, Issues, and Movements*. Rev. and exp. ed. New Brunswick: Rutgers University Press, 2020.

52. International Labour Organization, "ILO Constitution."

SOLIDARITY MOVEMENT

This is the duty of our generation as we enter the twenty-first century—solidarity with the weak, the persecuted, the lonely, the sick, and those in despair. It is expressed by the desire to give a noble and humanizing meaning to a community in which all members will define themselves not by their own identity but by that of others.

—Elie Wiesel

According to Hinde and Rotblat, "The abolition of war must depend on the work of international bodies, national groups, or large non-government organizations."[53] Perhaps the word "and" would have been more appropriate because solidarity is a collective effort by individuals, groups, *and* organizations with a common goal. The term "solidarity movement" has been associated with the Polish Union Movement, the New Ethiopia Movement, the International (Palestinian) Movement, and any others. However, the meaning of solidarity is much broader in scope and suggests that many people and groups have similar goals and that working collaboratively between and among groups will bring us closer to abolishing war. Jacobson and Brand-Jacobson stated that "the burgeoning global movement for social justice . . . also provided further evidence of increasing participation and activism on the part of citizens around the world working for the strengthening/building of democracy and the transformation/transcending of direct, structural and cultural violence."[54] Thus, no single individual, group, or organization by itself will bring us genuine world peace. All who want to end the scourge of war must come together and work toward that end.

53. Hinde and Rotblat, *War No More*, 191.
54. Galtung, *Searching for Peace*, 124.

Suggested Reading

Latoszek, Marek. "'Solidarity'—A Contribution to Social Movement Theory." *Polish Sociological Review* 153 (2006) 39–53.

SUE FOR PEACE

Suing for peace is an act by a warring nation to end hostilities and initiate a peace process. Suing for peace is usually initiated by the losing party to stave off an unconditional surrender and may sometimes be favorable to the winning nation, as prosecuting a war to a complete or unconditional surrender may be costly. However, pressing for peace may sometimes be started by the winning faction to end the war for several reasons, such as where additional conflict would not be in the perceived best interest of the winning party. In this case, demands might be made, or the two nations may agree to a "white peace" or a return to the status quo *ante bellum.*

TAPASYA

Connected to Gandhi's conception of *ahimsa, tapasya* ("arduous" and "austere") refers to the conscious suffering required to achieve transformational change through nonviolence. The term indicates not only the willingness to suffer, but the determination not to shift the burden of one's suffering to another person, especially an opponent. This act requires great courage and self-control—characteristics of people who adhere closely to nonviolent rules of engagement. As Barash and Webel noted, the courage required to willingly suffer for nonviolent action counters the common misunderstanding that practitioners of nonviolence are weak or cowardly. "The reality is precisely opposite."[55]

---

55. Barash and Webel, *Peace and Conflict Studies*, 641.

Suggested Reading

Behera, Anshuman, and Shailesh Nayak, eds. *Gandhi in the Twenty First Century: Ideas and Relevance*. 1st ed. Singapore: Springer Singapore, 2022. https://doi.org/10.1007/978-981-16-8476-0.
Duyndam, Joachim, et al., eds. *Sacrifice in Modernity: Community, Ritual, Identity from*. Leiden: Brill, 2017.

STRATEGIC PEACEBUILDING

This is a set of complementary practices aimed at transforming a society from a state of violence or deep injustice to one of greater just peace.[56] Applying a long-term framework that stretches across generations, strategic peacemaking engages both the immediate crisis and the building of cross-group relationships and alliances that will survive intermittent conflicts and create a basis for sustainable human security. Strategic peacebuilding may involve attempts to stop ongoing violence as well as strategies that advance sustainable peace and justice, such as monitoring of peace agreements, demobilization of armed groups, accountability for perpetrators, reconciliation, resettlement of displaced people, and economic development. Daniel Philpott and Gerard Powers wrote the seminal text on strategic peacebuilding—*Strategies of Peace: Transforming Conflict in a Violent World*—in 2010. Strategic peacebuilding continues to be a main focus on the work of the Kroc Institute for International Peace Studies at the University of Notre Dame Keough School of Global Affairs.

Suggested Reading

Kroc Institute for International Peace Studies. "Strategic Peacebuilding." https://kroc.nd.edu/research/strategic-peacebuilding/.
Philpott, Daniel, and Gerard F. Powers, eds. *Strategies of Peace: Transforming Conflict in a Violent World*. Oxford: Oxford University Press, 2010.

56. Kroc Institute, "Strategic Peacebuilding."

TRANSARMAMENT

If we take care of the means we are bound
to reach the end, sooner or later.

—Mahatma Gandhi

"Transarmament" is a term coined by Gene Sharp to describe a
process whereby the civilian population of a country is trained *en
masse* to use nonviolent means to repel an invader or to remove an
occupier. This training would be phased in over time as military
preparedness is phased out, until the citizenry is fully capable of defending the country without the use of arms. Unlike disarmament,
transarmament replaces military defense with nonviolent defense
rather than simply reducing or abandoning military capabilities.

Suggested Reading

Sharp, Gene. *National Security Through Civilian-Based Defense*. Omaha, NE:
Association for Transarmament Studies, 1985.

TRANSNATIONAL SOCIAL MOVEMENTS

These movements are social movements in which members from
different nations cooperatively engage in efforts to influence national policies and international relations. Transnational organizations—like the International Physicians for the Prevention of
Nuclear War (1980) and The Pugwash Conferences on Science
and World Affairs (1957)—can bring together experts from rival
nations who can agree on proposals and in turn, constructively
influence the political leaders of their respective countries. In his
1999 book, *Unarmed Forces: The Transnational Movement to End
the Cold War*, Matthew Evangelista makes the case that transnational groups played a significant role in bringing the Cold War to
an end, mainly by convening scientific experts from both sides to
talk about matters of common interest (the avoidance of nuclear

war) at a time when their respective governments were highly suspicious of such dialogue, and by using their influence as respected voices in their countries to influence the thinking of political leaders.

Suggested Reading

Guidry, John A., et al. *Globalizations and Social Movements: Culture, Power, and the Transnational Public Sphere.* Ann Arbor: University of Michigan Press, 2000.

Tarrow, Sidney G. *Power in Movement: Social Movements and Contentious Politics.* New York: Cambridge University Press, 2011. See especially chapter 12, "Transnational Contention," 234–58.

TRUTH AND RECONCILIATION COMMISSIONS

Truth and reconciliation commissions are transitional justice mechanisms established in the wake of conflict to investigate past atrocities or human rights violations, foster reconciliation, and prevent a recurrence of violence. Key aims of truth and reconciliation commissions include the following:

1. sanctioned fact finding
2. hear, respect, and respond to the needs of victims
3. improve accountability
4. evaluate institutional responsibility
5. promote reconciliation[57]

After the end of apartheid in South Africa, Bishop Desmond Tutu oversaw one of the most well-known commissions, South Africa's Truth and Reconciliation Commission (TRC). Barash describes South Africa's TRC as a significant example of country's attempt to deal with its violent past:

> The process, based on the African concept of *ubuntu*— social cohesion and shared goals and responsibility—was

57. Hayner, *Unspeakable Truths*, 20–23.

extraordinary, involving public testimony about abuses, intimidation, and murder, in the hopes of achieving national reconciliation.[58]

Desmond Tutu believed strongly that forgiveness and reconciliation occur in a *quid pro quo* context in that the perpetrator must admit to wrongs he has done and then apologize sincerely for them. To reciprocate and begin the healing process, the family members of the victims must forgive to complete the circle. However, forgiveness can be given even without contrition and confession. Tutu noted that "Jesus did not wait until those nailing him to the cross had asked for forgiveness. He was ready, as they drove in the nails, to pray to his father to forgive them."[59] For Tutu, not to forgive places the victim in a perpetual condition of victimhood. Forgiveness has the power to humanize people who have lost their humanity and heal those whose lives have been shattered by those who took the lives of their loved ones. Truth and reconciliation commissions have now been used around the world in an attempt to provide a way forward for societies impacted by gross violations of human rights.

Suggested Reading

Hayner, Priscilla. *Unspeakable Truths: Transitional Justice and the Challenge of Truth Commissions.* 2nd ed. New York: Routledge, 2010.

UNITED NATIONS (UN)

The UN is an intergovernmental organization founded in 1945, which includes a General Assembly (with representatives from 193 nations), a Security Council (with permanent members consisting of the US, Britain, China, France, and Russia), and an International Court of Justice. Nearly all power rests with the Security Council, which is empowered by the UN Charter to authorize

58. Barash, *Approaches to Peace*, 277.
59. Barash, *Approaches to Peace*, 279.

the use of sanctions including armed force to be drawn from the armed forces of member states. The UN also has many agencies to address a broad spectrum of needs in keeping with its purposes as stated in chapter 1, article 1 of its charter: "To achieve international co-operation in solving international problems of an economic, social, cultural, or humanitarian character, and in promoting and encouraging respect for human rights and for fundamental freedoms for all without distinction as to race, sex, language, or religion."[60]

Suggested Reading

UN. https://www.un.org/en/.

UN CONVENTION ON THE PREVENTION AND PUNISHMENT OF THE CRIME OF GENOCIDE

Passed in 1948 and ratified into international law in 1951, the UN Genocide Convention establishes a legal definition for the crime of genocide and makes genocide punishable according to international law. Based on the work of Raphael Lemkin, a Polish Jewish Juror who coined the term "genocide" in 1944, the final terms of the convention were a result of negotiation and political compromise by UN member states and the members of the UN drafting committee. The first three articles of the convention are worth quoting in full:

> Article I: The Contracting Parties confirm that genocide, whether committed in time of peace or in time of war, is a crime under international law which they undertake to prevent and to punish.

> Article II: In the present Convention, genocide means any of the following acts committed with intent to destroy, in whole or in part, a national, ethnical, racial or religious group, as such:
> (a) Killing members of the group;

60. UN, "United Nations Charter."

(b) Causing serious bodily or mental harm to members of the group;

(c) Deliberately inflicting on the group conditions of life calculated to bring about its physical destruction in whole or in part;

(d) Imposing measures intended to prevent births within the group;

(e) Forcibly transferring children of the group to another group.

Article III: The following acts shall be punishable:
(a) Genocide;
(b) Conspiracy to commit genocide;
(c) Direct and public incitement to commit genocide;
(d) Attempt to commit genocide;
(e) Complicity in genocide.[61]

Genocide scholars have criticized the UN Genocide Convention for its narrow interpretation of Lemkin's original definition, which focused on the identity-based targeting and cultural destruction of social collectivities (in contrast, the convention restricts its scope to four protected groups: national, racial, ethnic, and religious). Indeed, the convention has been applied only three times in prosecutions by international courts and tribunals since coming into force—in the case of the genocide against Cham Muslims and ethnic Vietnamese by the Khmer Rouge in Cambodia in the 1970s, the 1994 genocide against the Tutsi in Rwanda, and the 1995 genocide of Bosnian Muslims in Srebrenica. Even some of these judicial determinations are controversial because they exclude categories of victims such as class and political enemies targeted by the Khmer Rouge and Bosnian Muslims killed outside of Srebrenica. Another critique of the Convention, most recently articulated by A. Dirk Moses, is that it creates a hierarchy of atrocity crimes that has resulted in apathy toward cases of mass civilian destruction that are not driven by identity.[62] Despite its shortcomings, the Genocide Convention represents a significant

61. UN, "Convention on the Prevention."
62. Moses, "Fit for Purpose?"

legal foundation upon which scholars and human rights lawyers can build.

Suggested Reading

Waller, James. *Confronting Evil: Engaging Our Responsibility to Prevent Genocide*. New York: Oxford University Press, 2016.

UN GENERAL ASSEMBLY

The UN General Assembly is one of the two principal representative organs of the UN, and one in which all member nations have equal representation, viz. one vote. Its duties, as enshrined in chapter IV of the UN Charter, are to oversee the budget of the UN, appoint the non-permanent members to the Security Council, receive reports from UN agencies, and make recommendations in the form of General Assembly resolutions (which are not binding on member states). The General Assembly is headed by the secretary general, who is elected by the Assembly on nomination from the Security Council. The Assembly also can adopt certain treaties, opening them for member states' signatures and ratifications. More than 560 treaties have been adopted since the UN's beginning, covering issues such as disarmament, environmental protection, and human rights.[63]

Suggested Reading

UN. https://www.un.org/en/.

UN SECURITY COUNCIL

The UN Security Council is one of the principal organs of the UN, charged with the maintenance of international peace and security. Its duties, established by chapter VII of the UN Charter include

63. UN, "International Law and Justice."

the establishment of peacekeeping operations, the establishment of international sanctions, and the authorization of military action through Security Council resolutions. The Security Council is the only UN body with the authority to issue binding resolutions to member states. Like the UN itself, it was created to fix some of the shortcomings of its predecessor—the League of Nations. Of course, the Security Council, despite the potential power given to it under the Charter, has long been criticized for its own short-comings, especially the undemocratic veto power given to its five permanent members (the US, UK, France, China, and Russia).

Suggested Reading

UN. https://www.un.org/en/.

UNIVERSAL DECLARATION OF HUMAN RIGHTS (UDHR)

This declaration is a human rights instrument that came into being after the Second World War, committed to the inherent dignity of all human beings and to nondiscrimination. The UDHR was drafted by a UN committee headed by Eleanor Roosevelt and signed on December 10, 1948—one day after the UN Convention on the Prevention and Punishment of the Crime of Genocide. Altogether, it comprises thirty interconnected articles detailing economic, social, civil, political, and cultural rights to which all people are entitled. These include the right to work, the right to education, and the right to peaceful assembly. The authors of the UDHR believed that international commitment to the protection of human rights could fundamentally alter the global order. In article 28, they emphasized the importance of achieving "a social and international order in which the rights and freedoms set forth in this Declaration can be fully realized."[64] Although the UDHR is nonbinding, it has been signed by all 193 member states of the

---

64. UN, "Universal Declaration," art. 28.

UN and its provisions are considered by some legal analysts to be similar in weight to norms of customary international law.

Suggested Reading

UN. "Universal Declaration of Human Rights." https://www.un.org/en/about-us/universal-declaration-of-human-rights.

US INSTITUTE OF PEACE

The United States Institute of Peace (USIP) "is an independent, nonpartisan institution established and funded by Congress to increase the nation's capacity to manage international conflict without violence."[65] The campaign to establish the USIP began in the 1970s when the idea of a national peace academy was first brought to the Senate floor by a commission appointed by President Jimmy Carter. Congress formally established the Institute in 1984 under the administration of President Ronald Reagan, though it was not granted its permanent headquarters in Washington, DC, until 1996 when Congress authorized the Navy to transfer jurisdiction of a portion of its Potomac Annex facility on Navy Hill. USIP defines itself as a change agent, partnering with stakeholders to enact programs that promote the peaceful prevention, management, and resolution of international conflict. The Institute develops peacebuilding research, analysis, and educational tools for understanding global conflicts and applies the lessons learned in conflict zones around the world. Today, USIP operates in sixteen countries and has implemented programs in eighty-seven countries.

Suggested Reading

USIP. www.usip.org.

---

65. UN, "Universal Declaration," art. 28.

WORLD CITIZEN

The world is my country, all mankind are my brethren and to do good is my religion"

—THOMAS PAINE

The idea of a world citizen has a long history of uses dating back at
least as far as the ancient Greek philosopher Diogenes who, when
asked where he came from, replied, "I am a citizen of the world"
(see "Cosmopolitanism"). But perhaps the most famous notion of
world citizenship is associated with World War II veteran, peace
activist, and world federalist Garry Davis (1921–2013). In 1948, he
addressed the UN General Assembly calling for "one government
for one world." Later that year, after giving up his American citizenship, he gathered a crowd of twenty thousand in Paris to demand
that the UN recognize the rights of humanity (which it did in December of that year through the Universal Declaration of Human
Rights). While in Paris, Davis founded the International Registry of
World Citizens, which registered over 750,000 people by 1950. His
commitment to World Citizenship received support from many
distinguished peace activists, including Albert Einstein, Albert Camus, Andre Gide and Jean-Paul Sartre. In 1953, he declared (from
Ellsworth, Maine) the World Government of World Citizens and
organized the World Service Authority as its executive agency. The
agency went on to issue thousands of "world passports." The passports are not generally recognized as legal by most nations but have
been accepted on occasion by as many as 180 countries since 1954.
Their value has been mainly one of moral force, based, as Davis
often claimed, on the inalienable right to travel guaranteed by the
Universal Declaration of Human Rights.

Suggested Reading

Heater, Derek Benjamin. *World Citizenship: Cosmopolitan Thinking and Its Opponents*. New York: Continuum, 2002.

Kleingeld, Pauline. *Kant and Cosmopolitanism: The Philosophical Ideal of World Citizenship.* Cambridge: Cambridge University Press, 2012. https://doi.org/10.1017/CBO9781139015486.

WORLD COMMUNITY

Imagine all the people, living in peace. You may say that I'm a dreamer, but I'm not the only one. See I hope someday you'll join us, and the world be as one.

—JOHN LENNON

World community is a social philosophy that advocates for shared principles capable of underpinning a global society. It emphasizes humanity's shared responsibility for solving global problems and concepts like global citizenship. The philosophy of world community also champions coexistence and the ability of different cultures to thrive side by side. Fahey describes such a community as one that

> advocates the creation of an international democratic union of states that will abolish war, defend human rights, secure social justice, and protect the environment for future generations. . . . [A community] distinguished by the rule of international law that secures justice for all and guarantees human rights through a world charter that includes a bill of rights to protect political minorities from the tyranny of the majority.[66]

Other thinkers, such as Betty Reardon, have proposed world values that would similarly support such a global order. In 1988, Reardon wrote, "World order seeks not only nonviolent solutions to conflicts, but even more important, *just* solutions to conflicts."[67] She listed five values that express a just world order, which can be summarized as follows: the minimization of violence or war prevention; the maximizing of economic welfare; the increasing of social

---

66. Fahey, *War and the Christian,* 148.
67. Reardon, *Comprehensive Peace Education,* 4.

justice; increasing the participation of minorities and individuals in decision-making processes; and improving the quality of life through restoration of ecological balance.

Suggested Reading

Fahey, Joseph J. *War and the Christian Conscience*. Maryknoll, NY: Orbis, 2005.

WORLD CORE CURRICULUM

Robert Muller, former assistant secretary general of the UN, proposed a world core curriculum that consists of four major topics. These include: Our Planetary Home (the deserts, polar caps, biosphere, etc.); The Human Family (cultures, religions, etc.); Our Place in Time (our sun, globe, standards of living, levels of health, etc.); and The Miracle of Human Life (good physical lives, good mental lives, good moral lives, and good spiritual lives).[68] Referring to children who are born on the earth daily, Muller wrote, "The newcomers must be educated so that they can benefit from our acquired knowledge, skills and art of living, enjoy happy and fulfilled lives, and contribute in turn to the continuance, maintenance and further ascent of humanity or a well-preserved planet."[69] The idea was that peoples of the world should not only share their knowledge with each other, but they should also have access to the accumulated knowledge about the world. This will increase universal understanding and appreciation and underscore our common humanity—a necessary step for world peace and social justice.

Suggested Reading

Muller, Robert. "World Core Curriculum." http://robertmuller.org/rm/R1/World_Core_Curriculum.html.

68. Sweeney, *Peace Catalogue*, 134–39.
69. Sweeney, *Peace Catalogue*, 134.

WORLD COURT (SEE "INTERNATIONAL COURT OF JUSTICE")

WORLD GOVERNANCE

Mankind's desire for peace can be realized only
by the creation of a world government

—ALBERT EINSTEIN

The idea of world government is as old as that of international law and the nation state itself. The French monk Émeric Crucé proposed one of the earliest plans in 1623. The main idea was to obtain collective peace and security through a voluntary relinquishment of state sovereignty. He proposed a voluntary restructuring of the entire world order by which European states, Turkey, Persia, India, China, African kingdoms, the Pope's dominions, and the Palestine region would send representatives to a permanent council to make binding decisions regarding international relations and disputes based on majority rule. William Penn proposed a similar plan in 1693 by which the monarchs of Europe would form a union and submit their sovereignties to a parliament whose decisions would be carried by three-fourths majority vote. Interestingly, contrary to his Quaker scruples, he advocated that non-complying monarchs be coerced, if necessary, by the collective force of the majority. Crucé's and Penn's utopian ideas never got off the ground; no monarchs would voluntarily give up state sovereignty to such an international body. Even an international organization such as the UN faces challenges from members states who fear a weakening of their national sovereignty.

But the idea of world governance experienced an amazing rebirth in the five years following World War II, although some intellectuals like Bertrand Russell and Albert Einstein had given the notion unflagging support since World War I. World War II left the world with many times the destruction and carnage of the First

World War, including the advent of nuclear weapons. As Einstein and others put it, "The unleashed power of the atom has changed everything save our modes of thinking, and thus we drift toward unparalleled catastrophe."[70] A third world war would likely mean the destruction of world civilization, if not the human species itself, and many became convinced that some form of world governance that transcended state sovereignty was necessary to do that.

The most popular form of world government was that of a world federation that would have a monopoly on the major weapons of war (including nuclear weapons) and would allow member states to retain sovereignty in domestic affairs, except in building and maintaining weapons of war. One of the most carefully crafted plans for world government was laid out by legal scholars Clark and Sohn in their 1966 *World Peace Through World Law.* According to their plan, the UN would develop a democratic world government. It would include a security council with seventeen members; armed actions authorized by the council would require a two-thirds majority, including a majority of the four largest members (China, the US, the Soviet Union, India); there would be no veto; an inspection commission would oversee gradual total world disarmament at the rate of 10 percent a year of all nations; a world peace force under UN control would consist of approximately five hundred thousand volunteers and would gain armed force as world nations become disarmed; and it could access nuclear weapons via a UN nuclear authority.[71]

Today, many would find plans like those of Clark and Sohn wildly utopian if not downright dangerous. Even Einstein recognized the danger of such a powerful federation seizing control at the expense of human liberty. But he feared the risk of nuclear holocaust in this war prone system of sovereign states even more. And that greater fear was shared by millions worldwide at the end of the Second World War. For nearly five years, world governance organizations proliferated in the West, and popular opinion in scores of nations supported the idea of strict limitations on national

70. Wittner, "Einstein's Postwar Campaign."

71. See the proposed plan laid out in Clark and Sohn, *World Peace.*

sovereignty regarding the acquisition and use of national military force. The figures below, from Lawrence Wittner's 2012 book *One World or None*, show the remarkable levels of popular and national support for a world government in the late 1940s:

- Great Britain—a UN Educational, Scientific and Cultural Organization (UNESCO) poll showed that 44 percent of Britons favored World Government

- Canada—59 percent approval rate (The Canadian Institute for Public Opinion)

- France—45 percent approval rate (UNESCO); by mid-1949 there were two hundred world federalists in the French National Assembly

- Germany: 46 percent approval (UNESCO)

- Italy: a two-to-one approval rate (UNESCO)

- Denmark—votes taken in two towns in the late 1940s showed strong support for world government; 92 percent in Silkeborg and 77 percent in Brande

- Norway—48 percent approval rate (UNESCO)

- Netherlands—46 percent approval rate (UNESCO)[72]

As significant as these European attitudes in favor of world government were in the late 1940s, US sentiments were even more remarkable. A 1946 Roper Poll showed that 63 percent of Americans approved of world government. Consider also:

- The plan for "reforming the UN into a world federation" received the endorsement of dozens of respected US organizations including Americans for Democratic Action, American Veterans Committee, the General Federation of Women's Clubs, the National Grange, the Farmers' Union, the United Auto Workers, the Junior Chamber of Commerce, Young

---

72. Wittner, *One World or None*, 39–170.

Democrats, Young Republicans, and numerous religious groups.[73]

- By 1949 the United World Federalists had nearly fifty thousand members and 720 chapters.

- World Government Week was proclaimed by nine state governors and fifty city mayors.

- Twenty state legislatures passed resolutions endorsing world government.

- Ninety-one members of the US House of Representatives introduced legislation supporting world government as "the fundamental objective" of US foreign policy. The resolution gained 111 co-sponsors in the House and twenty-one in the Senate.[74]

Americans on record at the time as favoring world federalism included Albert Einstein, Edward Teller (atomic scientist), President Harry Truman, Robert Hutchins (chancellor of the University of Chicago), Owen Roberts (Supreme Court Justice), Walter Reuther (labor leader), William Fulbright (US Senator), and Owen D. Young (businessman).

Unfortunately, by 1950 the Cold War had gained momentum, the East and West became divided along ideological lines, and hopes for post-war cooperation with the Soviet Union evaporated and with them hopes for some form of effective world governance.

Suggested Reading

Wittner, Lawrence S. *Working for Peace and Justice: Memoirs of an Activist Intellectual.* Knoxville: University of Tennessee Press, 2012.

73. Wittner, *One World or None*, 70.
74. Wittner, *One World or None*, 55–79.

2

Peacemaking Individuals A–Z

Blessed are the peacemakers: for they shall
be called the children of God.

—MATTHEW 5:9, KJV

DESPITE THE MANY WARS that litter the chronicles of human history, our species has also produced remarkable peacemakers whose
commitment and achievements have influenced events around the
world. The following is but a representative sample of such peacemakers. Those marked with asterisks are also Nobel Peace Prize
recipients.

JANE ADDAMS* (1860–1935)

True peace is not merely the absence of war, it is the presence of justice.

—JANE ADDAMS

(Laura) Jane Addams was a pioneer social worker in the settlement
house movement, a peace activist, and the first American woman
to receive a Nobel Peace Prize (in 1931). She was the eighth of nine

children born to John Huy and Sarah Eber Addams in Cedarville, Illinois. Her father was a prosperous miller, local politician, state senator, and friend to Abraham Lincoln. Addams had a congenital spinal defect that limited her physical mobility. Although Addams's mother died in childbirth when she was two years old, her childhood instilled in her Christian values and a sense of social mission. She graduated from the Rockford Female Seminary as valedictorian and went on to study medicine until poor health ended her studies. Following intermittent hospital stays, she traveled and studied in Europe for nearly two years and spent another two years reading and writing.

When Addams was twenty-seven, she returned to Europe with Ellen Gates Starr. The two friends visited Toynbee Hall settlement house in East London, which provided services to poor industrial laborers. Inspired, Addams and Gates returned to America to found Hull House in the industrial west side of Chicago. Opened in 1889, it was the first settlement house in the US. Their expressed purpose was "to provide a center for a higher civic and social life; to institute and maintain educational and philanthropic enterprises and to investigate and improve the conditions in the industrial districts of Chicago."[1] Addams and Gates enlisted the help of young women from wealthy families to assist them. By its second year, Hull House was serving two thousand people. It expanded to include a kindergarten and day care for working mothers, a night school, art gallery, coffee house, gymnasium, swimming pool, a cooperative boarding club for girls, English language and acculturation classes for immigrants, a book bindery, art studio, music school, drama group, circulating library, and employment bureau, among other initiatives.

In 1905 Addams was appointed to Chicago's Board of Education and then made chairman of the School Management Committee. In 1908 she participated in the founding of the Chicago School of Civics and Philanthropy and the following year became the first woman president of the National Conference of Charities and Corrections. In her own area of Chicago she led investigations

1. Paul, "Jane Addams."

on midwifery, narcotics consumption, milk supplies, and sanitary conditions, even going so far as to accept the official post of garbage inspector of the Nineteenth Ward at an annual salary of one thousand dollars. In 1910, she received the first honorary degree ever awarded to a woman by Yale University. Addams believed strongly that women's voices should be heard particularly through their right to vote and she spread her beliefs as a prolific writer and lecturer.

Addams was a pacifist; during World War I she opposed America's entry into the war and became involved in international peacekeeping. She wrote *Newer Ideals for Peace* and *Peace and Bread in Times of War*, chaired the Women's Peace Party, and served as president of the International Congress of Women and the Women's International League for Peace and Freedom. Because of her opposition to World War I, she was vilified in the media and expelled from the Daughters of the American Revolution. Undaunted, she turned her efforts to assisting President Herbert Hoover in providing food relief supplies to the women and children of the enemy nations. In 1926, Addams suffered a heart attack that greatly diminished her health. She was later admitted to the hospital on December 10, 1931—the same day she and Nicholas Murray Butler were jointly awarded The Nobel Peace Prize—and subsequently diagnosed with cancer. She lived another four years, passing away on May 21, 1935.

Suggested Reading

Addams, Jane. "The Subtle Problems of Charity." *Atlantic Monthly* 83 (1899). https://www.theatlantic.com/magazine/archive/1899/02/the-subtle-problems-of-charity/306217/.

Elshtain, Jean Bethke. *The Jane Addams Reader*. New York: Basic, 2002.

The Nobel Prize. "Jane Addams Biographical." https://www.nobelprize.org/prizes/peace/1931/addams/biographical/.

SMEDLEY BUTLER (1881–1940)

War is a racket. It is the only one international in scope. It is the only one in which the profits are reckoned in dollars and the losses in lives.

—SMEDLEY BUTLER

Major General Smedley Darlington Butler, nicknamed "Old Gimlet Eye" and the "Fighting Quaker," attained the rank of major general in the US Marine Corps and won sixteen military medals (five for valor), including two Congressional Medals of Honor. He is one of only nineteen men to receive the Medal of Honor twice. After a long and storied military career, he became a vocal critic of war and American military intervention.

Butler fought in both the Mexican Revolution and World War I. He was born in West Chester, Pennsylvania and married to Ethel Conway Peters. Together, they had three children. He attended Haverford College where he was a gifted athlete and good student. Butler took part in operations around Guantanamo Bay, Cuba, and in the Philippine–American War, the Boxer Rebellion, and the Battle of Tientsin in China. While stationed in Puerto Rico, he was ordered to aid in protecting American interests during a revolt in Honduras. He took part in the bombardment, assault, and capture of Coyotepe, Honduras in October 1912. In 1914, he secured the city of Veracuz, Mexico during the Mexican Revolution. Butler also led a force on Haiti after a revolution threw the country into chaos. His victories over the Haitian rebels won him a second Medal of Honor, thereby being one of only two Marines to win the medal twice. He fought in France during World War II and later became commandant of the Marine base at Quantico, Virginia. Butler was known for his leadership and commitment to the welfare of the men under his command. He rose quickly through the ranks to become one of the youngest major generals at age forty-eight. After becoming a major general, he served as Director of Public Safety. But he longed for military life, so he went to China to command the Third Marine Expeditionary Brigade.

Butler retired from the military in 1931. By then, he was beginning to question US involvement in foreign conflicts. He had come to believe that war—in particular World War I—was really a profitable business for the few and at the expense of thousands of lives. He thought of himself as a cog in the imperialist war machine. After retiring from the Marines, he gave lectures around the country focusing his speeches against war profiteering and American military intervention abroad. The content of these lectures led to his 1935 work *War Is a Racket*, which showed the connections between war and business. Prior to World War II, Butler spoke out against what he saw as admiration for fascism and for Italy's leader Benito Mussolini. He was punished for telling an unfavorable story about Mussolini and avoided court-martial by accepting a reprimand. Because of his rank, he was able to write his own reprimand and never apologized to Mussolini. Throughout the 1930s, Butler continued to speak on these topics and on his views of fascism.

In June 1940, Butler entered the Philadelphia Naval Hospital after being ill for several weeks. On June 20, 1940 Butler died of cancer and was buried at Oaklands Cemetery in West Chester. At the time of his death, Butler was the most decorated Marine in US history. His activism against war inspired future veterans' movements for peace. The Boston chapter of Veterans For Peace is named the "Smedley D. Butler Brigade." Butler was also featured in the 2003 documentary *The Corporation*. He felt that three steps must be taken to smash the war racket: taking the profit out of war, permitting the youth of the land who would bear arms to decide whether there should be war, and limiting our military forces to home defense purposes.

Suggested Reading

Butler, Smedley D. *War Is a Racket*. New York: Round Table, 1935.

Schmidt, Hans. *Maverick Marine: General Smedley D. Butler and the Contradictions of American Military History*. Lexington: Kentucky University Press, 1998.

Streckler, Mark. *Smedley D. Butler, USMC: A Biography*. Jefferson, NC: McFarland, 2011.

HELEN CALDICOTT (1938-)

Patriotism is nationalism, and always leads to war.

—HELEN CALDICOTT

Helen Caldicott is an Australian physician and anti-nuclear activist. She spent time in the US at Children's Center Medical Hospital and taught pediatrics at Harvard's medical school in the late 1970s. In March 1979, a cooling malfunction caused a partial meltdown of a reactor core at the Three Mile Island nuclear power plant in Pennsylvania, releasing small amounts of radioactive gas into the environment. Shortly after this incident, Caldicott gave up her medical practice and began an international campaign against nuclear weapons and atomic energy. She founded the Women's Action for Nuclear Disarmament (WAND) in the US (later renamed Women's Action for New Directions). She served as president of the Physicians for Social Responsibility (PSR) from 1978 to 1983 and was instrumental in recruiting some twenty-three thousand physicians committed to public education on the dangers of nuclear energy. In 1985, PSR's umbrella organization, International Physicians for the Prevention of Nuclear War, received the Nobel Peace Prize. Caldicott herself received the Humanist of the Year award from the American Humanist Association in 1982. She has been featured in documentaries, including the 2004 documentary film *Helen's War: Portrait of a Dissident*. In 2012, The Smithsonian Institute named Caldicott as one of the most influential women of the twentieth century.

Suggested Reading

Caldicott, Helen. *Loving This Planet*. New York: New, 2012.
———. *Nuclear Power Is Not the Answer*. New York: Norton, 2006.

GARRY DAVIS (1921–2013)

The nation-state is a political fiction which perpetuates anarchy and is the breeding ground of war.

—GARRY DAVIS

In 1948, former Broadway actor and World War II B-17 bomber pilot Garry Davis renounced his US nationality as a personal action for world peace and declared himself a world citizen. Since then, the movement he set in motion has spread around the world. World citizenship has become central to a myriad of activities promoting global peace through world law.

Davis was a lifelong critic of nationalism and champion of the idea of world citizenship, at least since his 1948 address to the UN General Assembly (as a self-proclaimed world citizen) where he called for "one government for one world." Davis founded the World Government of World Citizens, which issued "world passports," visas, and birth certificates to oppose conflicts caused by national borders. Davis is known to have registered at least 950,000 people as world citizens. His ideas were enthusiastically received by many Europeans and Americans in the decade following World War II and an influence on peacemakers such as Albert Einstein. Davis was jailed at least thirty-two times in his life in protest of what he called "the violent lunacy of nationalism."[2] Davis died of cancer at the age of ninety-one. On his way to hospice, he attempted to convert his driver into a world citizen, handing him a copy of the UN Universal Declaration of Human Rights, which he was known to carry.

Suggested Reading

Davis, Garry. *A World Citizen in the Holyland.* South Burlington, VT: The World Government House, 1998.

Davis, Garry, and Greg Guma. *Passport to Freedom: A Guide for World Citizens.* Cabin John, MD: Seven Locks, 1992.

2. Chawkins, "Garry Davis."

DANIEL ELLSBERG (1931–2023)

There should be at least one leak like the Pentagon Papers every year.

—DANIEL ELLSBERG

Daniel Ellsberg, a Marine Vietnam combat veteran, gained national attention in 1971 when he released to the *New York Times* a top-secret study of the US intervention in Vietnam (known as "The Pentagon Papers") that he had done a few years earlier for the Pentagon. The study revealed serious distortions in the Lyndon B. Johnson administration's public record. Ellsberg felt a moral obligation to make the truth known to the American people and to the world. His act was one of nonviolent civil disobedience in the tradition of Gandhi and Martin Luther King Jr. The US government sued the *New York Times* and brought espionage charges against Ellsberg. But the Supreme Court upheld the *New York Times's* publication, and charges against Ellsberg were dismissed on grounds of government misconduct (illegal wiretapping and break-ins). Ellsberg continued to be politically active and outspoken. He was a vocal critic of the US invasion of Iraq and a longtime advocate for the abolition of nuclear weapons. He was a strong defender on grounds of conscience of other whistleblowers, including Chelsea (Bradley) Manning (who released State Department documents to WikiLeaks) and Edward Snowden (who released NSA documents to the *Guardian*).

Suggested Reading

Ellsberg, Daniel. *Papers on the War.* New York: Simon and Schuster, 1972.
Sheinkin, Steve. *Most Dangerous: Daniel Ellsberg and the Secret History of the Vietnam War.* New York: Roaring, 2015.
Wells, Tom. *Wild Man: The Life and Times of Daniel Ellsberg.* London: Palgrave Macmillan, 2001.

ERICH FROMM (1900–1980)

I believe that the man choosing progress can find a new
unity through the development of all his human forces,
which are produced in three orientations. These can be presented separately or together: biophilia [love of life], love for
humanity and nature, and independence and freedom.

—FROMM'S "HUMANIST CREDO"[3]

Erich Fromm was a psychoanalyst and social philosopher born
and educated in Germany. He left Germany after the Nazi takeover
in 1933 and settled in the US, where he wrote influential books
and served on the faculties of several schools, including Columbia
University, Bennington College, and Michigan State University.
One of his well-known works that set out the principles of his
humanistic and democratic socialism is *The Sane Society* (1955).
In it, Fromm argued that modern humans had become estranged
from themselves within industrial, consumer-driven society. Perhaps his most popular book, *The Art of Loving* (1956), became an
international bestseller. Fromm was a cofounder of the National
Committee for a Sane Nuclear Policy (SANE), an influential anti-
nuclear peace organization during much of the Cold War that later
merged with the Nuclear Weapons Freeze Campaign (FREEZE) to
become Peace Action (1993).

Suggested Reading

Fromm, Erich. *The Anatomy of Human Destructiveness*. New York: Open Road,
    1973.
———. *The Art of Loving*. New York: Harper, 1956.
———. *Escape from freedom*. New York: Farrar and Rhinehart, 1941.

3. Fromm, *Being Human*, 101.

MAHATMA GANDHI (1869–1948)

The world of tomorrow will be, must be, a society based on nonviolence.

—MAHATMA GANDHI

Mohandas Gandhi—often referred to as Mahatma (an honor-
ific Sanskrit word for "great-souled")—was born in India of the
Hindu faith and educated as a lawyer in England. Gandhi is best
known for his courageous and ultimately successful campaign of
nonviolent action against British rule in India. He began his work
with nonviolent civil disobedience in South Africa in the decade
before World War I to overcome discrimination against the Indian
minority. He returned to India in 1915 and undertook a three-
decade-long nonviolent struggle that led his country to independence from Britain shortly after World War II.

Gandhi's techniques and philosophy of nonviolence (see
"*ahimsa*" and "*satyagraha*" in chapter 1) have inspired movements across the globe for civil rights and freedom, including the
US struggle for civil rights in the 1950s and 1960s and the Arab
Spring. Although he never won, Gandhi was nominated for the
Nobel Peace Prize five times. Following his assassination in 1948,
the Nobel Peace Prize committee considered awarding it to him
posthumously but decided instead to withhold the Prize that year
on the grounds that there was no suitable living candidate.

Suggested Reading

Cortright, David. *Ghandi and Beyond: Nonviolence for a New Political Age*. 2nd
    ed. Boulder, CO: Paradigm, 2009.
Gandhi, Mohandas. *The Story of My Experiments with Truth: An Autobiography*.
    Uttar Pradesh, India: OM International, 1927.

THICH NHAT HANH (1926–2022)

To stop any suffering, no matter how small, is a great action of peace.

—THICH NHAT HANH

Born in Vietnam, Thich Nhat Hanh (pronounced "tic not hawn") became a Buddhist monk at the early age of sixteen. By age thirty he founded what became one of the best known Buddhist institutes in Vietnam. During the Vietnam War, amidst its devastating destruction to people and property, he developed "engaged Buddhism" whereby he and his fellow monks went out into the villages to share the teachings of the Buddha to bring solace and inner peace to a suffering population. They inspired ten thousand followers to help build hundreds of clinics and schools for some of the most severely devastated areas of the region. Tich Nhat Hanh traveled to the US during the war hoping to inspire a change in US policy. "The real enemy of man is not man. The real enemy is our ignorance, discrimination, fear, craving and violence," he stated.[4] In 1967 Martin Luther King Jr. nominated Thich Nhat Hanh for the Nobel Peace Prize. Tich Nhat Hanh died in 2022 at the age of ninety-five.

Suggested Reading

Hanh, Tich Nhat. *The Art of Power*. New York: Harper Collins, 2007.
———. *Being Peace*. Berkeley: Parallax, 1987.
———. *Peace Is Every Step: The Path of Mindfulness in Everyday Life*. New York: Bantam, 1991.

---

4. Beller and Chase, *Great Peacemakers*, 45–51.

DAISAKU IKEDA (1928–2023)

A great human revolution in just a single individual will help achieve a change in the destiny of a nation and, further, will enable a change in the destiny of humankind.

—Daisaku Ikeda

Daisaku Ikeda was a Japanese-born Buddhist philosopher, educator, author, and peacebuilder. When he was thirty-two, he became the third president of Soka Gakkai Buddhist organization, a grassroots movement empowering citizens. He also presided as president of Soka Gakkai International (SGI), which became one of the world's largest and most diverse lay Buddhist organizations with members in over 190 countries and territories. SGI promotes a philosophy of moral development and social engagement for peace. Ikeda's drive for peace was fueled by his experiences of World War II as a teenager, during which his brother was killed. Ikeda engaged in diplomatic dialogue with actors around the world in pursuit of peace. During the Cold War, he called for the normalization of relations between Japan and China. To promote global dialogue, he established independent institutes to further cross-cultural exchange and understanding. He developed the Soka educational system (catering to kindergarten through university students), which drew upon his belief in the infinite potential of each individual, the dignity of human life, and the belief that global peace is dependent on a self-directed transformation in an individual's life. He outlined his theory of global peace in his 2019 book *The Human Revolution*. Ikeda died in Japan in 2023 at the age of ninety-five.

Suggested Reading

Ikeda, Daisaku. *Hope Is a decision.* Santa Monica, CA: Middleway, 2017.
———. *The Human Revolution.* Santa Monica, CA: World Tribune, 2019.
———. *Wisdom for Creating Happiness and Peace.* Santa Monica, CA: World Tribune, 2015.

LÉON JOUHAUX* (1879–1954)

I would not go so far as to say that the French trade unions attached greater importance to the struggle for peace than the others did; but they certainly seemed to take it more to heart.

—LÉON JOUHAUX

Léon Jouhaux was a French labor leader who became the secretary general of France's General Confederation of Labour in 1909, a position he held until 1947. Jouhaux's work with the union started at a young age. When he was sixteen, he dropped out of secondary school and worked for the same match factory as his father after a strike suspended his father's wages. In his long career as a labor leader, he was instrumental in gaining workers' rights in France, including the eight-hour work day, collective bargaining, paid holidays, and the right to union representation.

Jouhaux initially opposed France's entry into World War II, organizing several mass protests, but supported France's war efforts and the defeat of Nazi Germany once the war began. Jouhaux was arrested and imprisoned in Buchenwald concentration camp, and later the Castle Itter, before being freed in 1945.

After the war, Jouhaux formed the social-democrat Workers' Force (CGT-FO). He served in several international trade union bodies, including the International Federation of Trade Unions, and was instrumental in the establishment of the International Labour Organization (ILO). Jouhaux was awarded the Nobel Peace Prize in 1951. He died in 1954 in Paris and is interred in Le Père Lachaise Cemetery.

Suggested Reading

Jouhaux, Léon. "Nobel Lecture" The Nobel Prize. https://www.nobelprize.org/prizes/peace/1951/jouhaux/lecture/.

MARTIN LUTHER KING JR.* (1929–1968)

Nonviolence is not sterile passivity, but a powerful moral force which makes for social transformation.

—MARTIN LUTHER KING JR.

Martin Luther King Jr. was an American Baptist minister and civil rights leader. It was largely through the civil rights movement inspired and led by King in the 1950s and 1960s that the racial injustices of the segregated South were successfully challenged and great advances were made towards racial equality in the US. King was an advocate and practitioner of nonviolent civil disobedience in the tradition of Henry David Thoreau and Mahatma Gandhi. Like Gandhi and Thoreau, he was often arrested and jailed for acts of nonviolent civil disobedience. He was also an outspoken critic of the American role in the Vietnam War and urged young men to refuse to obey the draft on grounds of conscience. King was awarded the Nobel Peace Prize in 1964 at the age off thirty-five—the youngest ever recipient at that time. He was assassinated in 1968 while standing on the balcony of his hotel room in Memphis, Tennessee.

Suggested Reading

Bill of Rights Institute. "Letter from Birmingham Jail." https://billofrightsinstitute.org/primary-sources/letter-from-birmingham-jail.
NPR. "Read Martin Luther King Jr.'s 'I Have a Dream' Speech in Its Entirety." https://www.npr.org/2010/01/18/122701268/i-have-a-dream-speech-in-its-entirety.

DALAI LAMA TENZIN GYATSO* (1935–)

Hard times build determination and inner strength. Through them we can also come to appreciate the uselessness of anger. Instead of getting angry, nurture a deep caring and respect for troublemakers because by creating such trying circumstances they provide us with invaluable opportunities to practice tolerance and patience.

—DALAI LAMA

Dalai Lama Tenzin Gyatso is the fourteenth Dalai Lama—the Tibetan Buddhist spiritual and political leader—since the four-teenth century. In 1959, after a decade of Chinese intervention and oppression, he was forced to flee to India where he established a government in exile. Although China's expropriation of Tibet was condemned by the international community as a criminal violation of human rights, Tibet remains under Chinese control today. For more than half a century the Dalai Lama has traveled the world seeking justice for Tibet and spreading his message of peace and nonviolence. The Dalai Lama received the Nobel Peace Prize in 1989.

Suggested Reading

Dalai Lama. *Essential Teachings*. Berkeley: North Atlantic, 1985.
———. *How to Practice: The Way to a Meaningful Life*. New York: Pocket, 2002.
Dalai Lama, and Howard C. Cutler. *The Art of Happiness: A Handbook for Living*. New York: Riverhead, 1998.

NELSON MANDELA* (1918–2013)

If you want to make peace with your enemy, you have to work with your enemy. Then he becomes your partner.

—NELSON MANDELA

Nelson Mandela was a South African anti-apartheid political leader who actively and courageously opposed the racist apart-heid regime in South Africa in the 1950s and early 1960s. In 1964, Mandela was sentenced to life in prison for his political activism against the regime. He was released in 1990 after serving twenty-seven years. He led the movement that successfully and nonvio-lently ended apartheid. In 1994, Mandela won the first universal (biracial) elections in South Africa and became the country's first black president. In 1993, Mandela (and F. W. de Klerk, then president with whom negotiations for biracial elections and a nonviolent end to apartheid were held) received the Nobel Peace Prize.

Suggested Reading

Mandela, Nelson. *In His Own Words*. New York: Little, Brown, 2003.
———. *The Long Walk to Freedom: The Autobiography on Nelson Mandela*. New York: Little, Brown, 1995.

PHILIP J. NOEL-BAKER* (1889–1982)

In the age when the atom has been split, the moon encircled, diseases conquered, is disarmament so difficult a matter that it must remain a distant dream?

—PHILLIP J. NOEL-BAKER

Philip J. Noel-Baker was an Englishman who won the Nobel Peace Prize in 1959 for his work on disarmament during the 1907 Hague International Peace Conference where the great powers met and negotiated agreements on disarmament and arbitration. He blamed the private arms manufacturers for inciting World War I so they could benefit financially. During the war he was a volunteer medical orderly. Afterward, he worked at the League of Nations. Noel-Baker studied history and law at Cambridge University. When World War II broke out, he became a minister in Winston Churchill's coalition government. He helped draft the UN Charter and worked tirelessly for the rest of his life to prevent war between the US and the Soviet Union.

Suggested Reading

Noel-Baker, Philip. *The Arms Race*. London: Atlantic, 1958.

LORD (JOHN) BOYD ORR OF BRECHIN*(1880-1971)

Recognize the common brotherhood of man and follow the example of the great Prince of Peace in feeding the hungry, relieving misery and disease, and there will be such a new spirit in the world that the very thought of war would be abhorrent.

—LORD BOYD ORR

Lord Boyd Orr won the Nobel Peace Prize in 1949. Born in Scotland, he was a British citizen who served as president of the National Peace Council and World Union of Peace Organizations, was a prominent organizer and director of the General Food and Agricultural Organization, and an alimentary politician, biologist, and physician. His major areas of focus included humanitarian work and world organizing. Considered the father of the Food and Agriculture Organization (FAO), Orr was concerned about the high level of malnutrition of many British citizens—a condition he attributed to low incomes. This prompted him to serve in the League of Nations where he helped draft an international policy on nutrition. Later, he presented the idea of a world food plan to President Franklin D. Roosevelt. Arguing that food and prosperity were the foundations of world peace, Orr was elected director-general of the Food and Agriculture Organization (FAO) established under the UN. Orr was also an ardent advocate for world government and international law. He believed that absolute national sovereignty undermined the interdependence of nations.

Suggested Reading

Boyd Orr, J. *As I Recall: The 1880s to the 1960s.* London: MacGibbon & Kee, 1966.
———. *Feast and Famine: The Wonderful World of Food.* London: Rathbone, 1957.

SR. HELEN PREJEAN (1939-)

In sorting out my feelings and beliefs, there is, however, one piece of moral ground of which I am absolutely certain: if I were to be murdered I would not want my murderer executed. I would not want my death avenged. Especially by government—which can't be trusted to control its own bureaucrats or collect taxes equitably or fill a pothole, much less decide which of its citizens to kill.

—SR. HELEN PRAJEAN

Sr. Helen Prejean was born in Baton Rouge, Louisiana and is a member of the Sisters of St. Joseph of Medaille (Congregation of St. Joseph). She has a bachelor of arts degree in English and education and a master of arts degree in religious education. Prajean has served as the religious education director at St. Frances Cabrini Parish in New Orleans and the formation director for her religious community. She has also taught at the junior and senior high school levels.

Prajean's prison ministry began in 1981, at which time she decided to dedicate her life to the poor of New Orleans. At one point in her life, she exchanged correspondence with Patrick Sonnier, a convicted killer who was sentenced to die in the electric chair of Louisiana's Angola State Prison. Prajean took Sonnier under her wing and her prison visits with him made her aware of the Louisiana execution process. This experience resulted in her *New York Times* bestseller *Dead Man Walking: An Eyewitness Account of the Death Penalty*. The book was also an international bestseller (it was translated into ten different languages) and was adapted into the film *Dead Man Walking*.

Prajean lectures widely and is a tireless advocate for the repeal of the death penalty. She is a member of several organizations devoted to the abolition of the death penalty and has been the chairperson of the board of the National Coalition to Abolish the Death Penalty. Prajean has witnessed several executions and continues to counsel not only the inmates on death row but also the families of their victims.

Suggested Reading

Prajean, Helen. *Dead Man Walking*. New York: Vintage, 1995.

———. *The Death of Innocents*. New York: Random House, 2006.

———. *River of Fire: My Spiritual Journey*. New York: Random House, 2019.

LINUS PAULING* (1901–1994)

Science is the search for truth—it is not a game in which one tries to beat his opponent, to do harm to others. We need to have the spirit of science in international affairs, to make the conduct of international affairs the effort to find the right solution, the just solution of international problems, not the effort by each nation to get the better of other nations, to do harm to them when it is possible.

—LINUS PAULING

A world-famous chemist and peace activist, Linus Pauling is the only person to have received two unshared Nobel Prizes. He received the Prize in Chemistry for work on the nature of chemical bonding in 1954 and he received the Peace Prize in 1963 for his work over several years to secure a treaty banning nuclear testing. The 1963 Partial Test Ban Treaty, ratified by the Soviet Union, the US, and the UK, banned all nuclear testing except for underground testing. The treaty's ban on atmospheric testing was especially important given the accumulating evidence of radioactive fallout entering the food chain and its deleterious and cancer-causing effects on living things.

Suggested Reading

Marinacci, Barbara, ed. *Linus Pauling: In His Own Words*. New York: Touchstone, 1995.

Pauling, Linus, and Daisaku Ikeda. *A Lifelong Quest for Peace*. Boston: Jones & Bartlett, 1990.

LUDWIG QUIDDE* (1858–1941)

The security of which we speak is to be attained by the development of international law through an international organization based on the principles of law and justice.

—LUDWIG QUIDDE

Ludwig Quidde, a German citizen, won the Nobel Peace Prize in 1927 for his lifetime of work towards peace. He shared the Peace Prize with Ferdinand Buisson of France. Quidde was a participant in numerous peace conferences, a member of the German Parliament, and professor at Berlin University. His areas of focus were negotiation and the peace movement. Despite having a doctorate in history, his opposition to the German kaiser prevented him from receiving official appointments. As a member of the International Peace Bureau, he attempted to lessen the enmity between Germany and France after the Franco-German war in 1870–1871.

Quidde was elected to the German Reichstag in 1907 and later became president of the German Peace Society, a post he held for fifteen years. During World War I he was outspoken in his condemnation of Germany's annexation of territory from neighboring countries, and for this he was placed under government watch. Even though Quidde was displeased by the harsh treatment of Germany after the war, he continued to work against Germany's pursuit of *lebensraum*. In 1894, Quidde wrote a satire on Emperor Wilhelm II and Prussian society entitled *Caligula: A Study of Imperial Insanity* based on Roman emperor Caligula who had a reputation for madness, abuse of power, and vanity. He was not found guilty of wrongdoing due to the difficulty of proving the pamphlet was any more than it appeared to be—a spoof of Caligula.

Quidde helped to form the German People's Party in 1895. Its political orientation was anti-war and anti-Prussian. For one of his political speeches in 1896, he received a three-month sentence in Stadelheim prison on the charge of lèse majesté. He was again sent to prison in 1924 for his critique on secret military training. The charge was collaborating with the enemy. Quidde had high ethical ideals, a strong distrust of the military, and a wife supportive of his work for peace. He fled to Switzerland when Hitler came into power and lived there for the remainder of his life. While in exile, he remained active by attending World Peace Congresses, publishing articles, and founding the Comité de Secours aux Pacifistes Exilés to take care of political exiles from Nazi Germany. He was never able to finish his book, *German Pacifism During the World War.*

Suggested Reading

Quidde, Ludwig. *The Kaiser's Double.* London: W. Rider, 1915. http://catalog. hathitrust.org/api/volumes/oclc/12963169.html.

BERTRAND RUSSELL (1872–1970)

It is obvious that modern war is not good for business from a financial point of view. Although we won both the world wars, we should now be much richer if they had not occurred.

—BERTRAND RUSSELL

Russell was a British philosopher, the grandson of twice Prime Minister John Russell. He was a mathematician and philosopher by training, but he wrote eighty books making valuable contributions in the fields of science, psychology, education, history, and politics. He was in some ways shaken out of his ivory scholastic tower by the upheavals of World War I and the widespread popular support in Britain for the war. Although he was not an absolute pacifist, he actively opposed the war and Britain's participation in it—actions for which he lost his teaching position at Cambridge and was sentenced to six months in prison.

Politically, Russell was of a democratic socialist inclination. He was one of the first Westerners to visit the Soviet Union after the 1917 revolution, and he wrote about it in his *Theory and Practice of Bolshevism* for which he was criticized by both communists and capitalists; while he didn't like the brutality and intolerance of the Bolsheviks, neither did he like the economic inequality of the "free market" system. For the rest of his life Russell was an outspoken critic of the nation-state and its war culture and was an early advocate of world government as the best solution for the security of international peace.

For a while, Russell opposed a war against Hitler and favored, for Britain, nonviolent resistance. But like Einstein, he reluctantly came to believe that force was unavoidable, and in 1941 he supported the war against Germany. After World War II, when the US alone had the atomic bomb, Russell had high hopes that a world government with a monopoly on the weapons of war could be formed, the spread of nuclear weapons prevented, and a third world war prevented. When the Soviets showed reluctance to cooperate with such international plans, Russell, for a brief time, advocated threatening the Soviets with war unless they agreed to such a scheme for international controls. Russell believed that such a threat would likely succeed without war. As international tensions in Europe increased and it became less certain that the Soviets would accede to Western ultimatums, Russell abandoned his idea. When the Soviets developed their own atom bomb (1949) and a nuclear arms race was in full swing, he set to work to ease Cold War tensions and, with Albert Einstein, to educate the world about the imminent dangers of nuclear annihilation (see "Russell–Einstein Manifesto"). The East and the West, they said, had an overriding common cause despite their seemingly irreconcilable ideological divide—the continued existence of the human species—"Remember your humanity and forget the rest."[5]

Russell was also a co-founder and first president of the Campaign for Nuclear Disarmament (CND, 1958). Indeed, CND's logo, the "peace symbol," is known worldwide. At the age of eighty-nine, Russell was imprisoned for the second time for his opposition against British nuclear weapons. During the Cuban Missile Crisis, he exchanged a series of telegrams with both John F. Kennedy and Nikita Khrushchev, imploring them to back away

5. Russell, "Russell–Einstein Manifesto," 2.

from the brink of nuclear war. In the 1960s, Russell was an early and vociferous critic of the Vietnam War and, with French philosopher Jean Paul Sartre, organized the International War Crimes Tribunal in Stockholm, Sweden and in Copenhagen, Denmark (1967). The Tribunal, consisting of twenty-eight notables, including several Nobel laureates from eighteen countries, received evidence concerning US war crimes in Vietnam. Russell died in 1970 in Wales at the age of ninety-seven.

Suggested Reading

Russell, Bertrand. *The Autobiography of Bertrand Russell*. Crows Nest, Australia: Allen & Unwin, 1971.
———. *Selected Papers of Bertrand Russell*. New York: Modern Library, 1955.

ÓSCAR ARIAS SÁNCHEZ* (1940–)

War, and the preparation of war, are the two greatest obstacles to human progress. The poor of the world are crying out for schools and doctors, not guns and generals.

—ÓSCAR ARIAS SÁNCHEZ

Óscar Arias Sánchez, former president of Costa Rica, received the Nobel Peace Prize in 1987 for brokering a peace treaty that brought peace to Central America at a time when countries in the region were engaged in civil strife that took the lives of thousands. Death squads flourished; political opponents were tortured and killed; and military oppression was widespread. In addition to Costa Rica, the peace plan was approved by Guatemala, El Salvador, Honduras, and Nicaragua. It called for free elections, human rights assurances, and an end to foreign meddling in the internal affairs of these countries.

Costa Rica itself was peaceful; it's former president, General José Figueres, had abolished the Costa Rican military in 1948. This enabled Sánchez to say, "Mine is an unarmed people . . . our children go with books under their arms, not with rifles on their shoulders."[6] One of his first acts in office was to eject US military advisors and Contras from his country, insisting that Costa Rica would not be used for military purposes. Sánchez significantly reduced poverty in Costa Rica by using money no longer spent on the military and putting it towards human development.

Suggested Reading

Cox, Vicki. *Oscar Arias Sánchez: Bringing Peace to Central America*. Broomall, PA: Chelsea House, 2007.

Sanchez, Oscar Arias. *Horizons of Peace*. San José, Costa Rica: Arias Foundation of Peace and Human Progress, 1994.

HENRY DAVID THOREAU (1817-1862)

If the machine of government is of such a nature that it requires you to be the agent of injustice to another, then, I say, break the law.

—HENRY DAVID THOREAU

Henry David Thoreau was an American essayist, poet, practical philosopher, New England Transcendentalist, and author of the book *Walden*. He was also an abolitionist, naturalist, and a strong believer in civil disobedience. His writing on nonviolence inspired Mahatma Gandhi, Martin Luther King Jr., and many others. He is also an inspiration for contemporary naturalists and environmentalists because of his communion with and study of nature during his two-year stay in a small cabin on Walden Pond in Concord, Massachusetts. After graduating from Harvard University, Thoreau developed a friendship with Ralph Waldo Emerson and became acquainted with Transcendentalism, a school of thought that emphasized the importance of empirical thinking and of spiritual matters over the physical world. At his small cabin on Walden Pond, Thoreau sought the simple life and worked at a pace that was slower than conventional practice. He worked in a pencil factory

6. Beller and Chase, *Great Peacemakers*, 62.

and as a land surveyor. He wanted to avoid situations where "the mass of men lead lives of quiet desperation."[7]

Thoreau was also an opponent of corporal punishment, slavery, the military, and conformity to society in general. He was a strong proponent of individual conscience, indicated in his statement, "The only obligation which I have a right to assume is to do at any time what I think right."[8] One of the incidents that epitomizes Thoreau's nonconformity was his refusal to pay the poll tax that he saw as financing the Mexican–American war. For this, he spent a night in jail. His experience led him to write his famous essay "Resistance to Civil Government" (later, *Civil Disobedience*), an essay that continues to inspire peacemakers throughout the world. Thoreau was also highly committed to abolishing slavery and wrote an article entitled "Slavery in Massachusetts." Thoreau died of tuberculosis in 1862 but his legacy makes him immortal.

Suggested Reading

Thoreau, Henry David. "Resistance to Civil Government." In *Æsthetic*, edited by Elizabeth P. Peabody, 189–211. Boston: Putnam, 1849. Reprint Floating, 2008.
———. *Walden*. New York, Crowell, 1854. Reprint, Floating, 2008.

WILLIAM URY (1953–)

When you are angry, you will make the best speech you will ever regret.

—WILLIAM URY

William Ury is a world leader in negotiation and mediation. He cofounded Harvard University's "Program on Negotiation" and is the author of multiple books, including *Getting to Yes*, which he cowrote with Roger Fisher in 1981. The book sold eight million

---

7. Thoreau, *Walden*, 8.
8. Thoreau, "Resistance to Civil Government," 190.

copies and has been translated into over thirty languages. It has been described as a leading authority on dispute resolution.

Over the last thirty years, Ury has served as a negotiation adviser and mediator in conflicts ranging from corporate mergers to wildcat strikes in a Kentucky coal mine and ethnic wars in the Middle East, the Balkans, and the former Soviet Union. With former President Jimmy Carter, he cofounded the International Negotiation Network, a non-governmental body seeking to end civil wars around the world. During the 1980s, he helped the US and Soviet governments create nuclear crisis centers designed to avert an accidental nuclear war. In that capacity, he served as a consultant to the Crisis Management Center at the White House. Ury has served as a third party in helping to end a civil war in Aceh, Indonesia, and helping to prevent civil war in Venezuela. He has taught negotiation skills to corporate executives, labor leaders, diplomats, and military officers around the world and is the co-founder of e-Parliament, which provides the twenty-five thousand members of congress and parliament around the world with an internet-based forum through which they can attempt to solve global problems such as climate change and energy efficiency.

In 2026, Ury founded the Abraham Path Initiative, which aims to build bridges between cultures and faiths through walking trails and cultural routes in the Middle East that retrace the footsteps of Abraham. Ury won the Whitney North Seymour Award from the American Arbitration Association and the Distinguished Service Medal from the Russian Parliament. He is a social anthropologist, with a bachelors of arts degree from Yale University and a doctor of philosophy degree from Harvard university. His research on negotiation spans from boardrooms and bargaining tables to the Bushmen of the Kalahari and the clan warriors of New Guinea.

Suggested Reading

Fisher, Roger, and William Ury. *Getting to Yes*. New York: Penguin, 1981.

Ury, William. *Getting to Peace: Transforming Conflict at Home, at Work, and in the World*. New York: Viking, 1999.

Ury, William, and James C. Collins. *Possible: How We Survive (and Thrive) in an Age of Conflict*. 1st ed. New York: Harper Business, 2024.

OSWALD GARRISON VILLARD (1872–1949)

What was criminal in Coventry, Rotterdam, Warsaw, and London has now become heroic in Dresden and now Tokyo.

—OSWALD GARRISON VILLARD

Oswald Garrison Villard, born in Wiesbaden, Germany, was an American journalist and editor of *The Nation* magazine. He was a leading liberal of the twentieth century, famous for his uncompromising commitment to pacifism and his advocacy for minority rights. Villard's father was an American newspaper correspondent and an immigrant from Germany; his mother was the daughter of abolitionist William Lloyd Garrison and a suffragist in her own right, co-founder of the Women's Peace Movement. Villard was educated at private schools and Harvard University. After serving a short apprenticeship at a Philadelphia paper, he joined the staff of his father's paper, the *New York Evening Post*. He quickly achieved editorial prominence at the paper and became owner and publisher after his father's death.

Villard was a strong opponent of the Spanish–American War, which he saw as imperialistic. He became a pacifist and supporter of women's rights. In addition, he advocated for the rights of African Americans, Jews, and other minorities as well as the rights of workers to form labor unions. He opposed US participation in World War I and viewed the subsequent Treaty of Versailles as unjust. Later, he supported Franklin D. Roosevelt's "New Deal." His opposition to military aid to the Allied forces in 1940 led to the cancellation of his articles by *The Nation*. Even after the attack on Pearl Harbor, Villard opposed World War II, thereby isolating himself further from conventional thinking. He died in New York City, never wavering in his beliefs and principles.

Suggested Reading

Humes, D. Joy. *Oswald Garrison Villard: Liberal of the 1920s*. Whitefish, MT: Literary Licensing, 2012.

Villard, Oswald G. *Fighting Years: Memoirs of a Liberal Editor*. New York: Harcourt, Brace, 1939.

JODY WILLIAMS* (1950-)

The landmine cannot tell the difference between a soldier or a civilian— a woman, a child, a grandmother going out to collect firewood to make the family meal . . . once peace is declared the landmine does not recognize that peace. The landmine is eternally prepared to take victims.

—JODY WILLIAMS

Jody Williams was born in Putney, Vermont. She studied international politics in college, and this inspired her to become involved in aid work in El Salvador where land mines covered the country and threatened the lives of civilians daily. One of her tasks was to provide prosthetic devices to children who had lost their limbs. This experience motivated her to campaign against land mines at the international level. Thus, the International Campaign to Ban Land Mines came into being and gained a membership of one thousand organizations from sixty countries. Due to Williams's efforts, the Ottawa Convention (Land Mine Treaty) was signed by 120 countries in 1999. In addition to banning the use, production, sale, and stockpiling of antipersonnel mines, it also contained provisions concerning mine clearance and the obligation to provide humanitarian assistance. Williams received the Nobel Peace Prize in 1997 for her work in the banning and clearing of antipersonnel mines. She continued to write and speak on the topic of land mines and has worked closely with governments and agencies throughout the world to rid the planet of land mines.

Suggested Reading

Williams, Jody. *Banning Landmines: Disarmament, Citizen Diplomacy, and Human Security.* NY: Roman & Littlefield, 2008.

———. *My Name Is Jody Williams: A Vermont Girl's Winding Path to the Nobel Peace Prize.* Berkeley: University of California, 2013.

LIU XIAOBO* (1955–2017)

Free expression is the base of human rights, the root of human nature and the mother of truth. To kill free speech is to insult human rights, to stifle human nature and to suppress truth.

—LIU XIAOBO

Liu Xiaobo was an outspoken Chinese intellectual and human rights advocate who was a strong critic of the Chinese communist government. He was detained, put under house arrest, and imprisoned numerous times for his writing and activism. A prolific writer, Xiaobo wrote nearly eight hundred essays and was a key drafter of Charter 08, a manifesto initially signed by over three hundred Chinese dissident intellectuals and human rights activists and published in 2008, the sixtieth anniversary of the Universal Declaration of Human Rights.

Xiaobo was born on December 28, 1955 in Changchun, Jilin. He received a bachelor of arts in literature from Jilin University and a master of arts and doctor of philosophy from Beijing Normal University where he later taught. Xiaobo left a position as a visiting scholar at Columbia University to participate in the 1989 Democracy Movement in Beijing. He and others went on a hunger strike in Tiananmen Square to protest martial law and attempt to mediate a peaceful resolution between the students and the government. Xiaobo was arrested, held in Beijing's Qincheng Prison, and later found guilty of counter-revolutionary propaganda and incitement. In 1996, he was sentenced to three years of reeducation through labor on charges of rumormongering, slander, and disturbing social order. In 2009, he was found guilty of inciting subversion of state power. In a show of support, more than six hundred co-signers of Charter 08 signed a statement of shared responsibility for Xiaobo's crime. Between 2003 and 2007, Xiaobo was president of the Independent Chinese PEN Center and a visiting scholar at the University of Oslo and the University of Hawaii. He was married to poet and visual artist Liu Xia.

Suggested Reading

Xiaobo, Liu. *A Single Blade and Toxic Sword: Critique on Contemporary Chinese Nationalism.* Sunnyvale, CA: Broad, 2006.

———. *No Enemies, No Hatred: Selected Essays and Poems.* Cambridge: Belknap, 2012.

MALALA YOUSAFZAI (1997–)

We realize the importance of our voices only when we are silenced.

Malala Yousafzai is a Pakistani activist for girls' right to education. Born to a social activist and educator, Yousafzai began her career as an activist at a young age. In 2007, the Tehrik-e Taliban Pakistan (TTP) invaded the Swat valley where Yousafzai and her family were living. They imposed Islamic law, shut down or destroyed girls' schools, and barred women from taking part in society. One year later, at the age of eleven, Yousafzai, whose family had fled the region, gave her first speech to a local press club in Peshwar, protesting the closing of schools. Yousafzai's speech—"How Dare the Taliban Take Away My Basic Right to Education?"—was published throughout Pakistan. In 2009, Yousafzai began blogging regularly about life under the Taliban for the BBC and made several television appearances. In 2011, she received Pakistan's first National Youth Peace Prize (later retitled the National Malala Peace Prize).

Yousafzai became a globally recognized figure in 2012 when she survived being shot in the head by the TTP on her way home from school. Worldwide protests against the assassination attempt led to the ratification of Pakistan's Right to Education bill and the establishment of a $10 million education fund in Yousafzai's honor. The Vital Voices Global Partnership created the Malala Fund to support education for girls around the world. Since surviving the attempt on her life, Yousafzai has continued to be an outspoken voice for children's rights and girls' education. She was named one of *Time* magazine's most influential people in 2013, coauthored a memoir titled *I Am Malala: The Girls Who Stood Up for Education and Was Shot by the Taliban,* and authored a children's book called *Malala's Magic Pencil.* Yousafzai received the Nobel Peace Prize in 2014 along with Kailash Satyarthi for their work on behalf of children's rights. Yousafzai was the youngest Nobel laureate to ever receive the prize. The following year, in partnership with the Malala Fund, Yousafzai opened a girls' school i Lebanon to serve refugees from the Syrian Civil War.

Suggested Reading

Yousafzai, Malala, and Patricia McCormick. *I Am Malala: How One Girl Stood up for Education and Changed the World.* Young readers ed. New York: Little, Brown, 2014.

HOWARD ZINN (1922–2010)

Civil disobedience is not our problem. Our problem is civil obedience. Our problem is that people all over the world have obeyed the dictates of leaders . . . and millions have been killed because of this obedience. . . . Our problem is that people are obedient all over the world in the face of poverty and starvation and stupidity, and war, and cruelty. Our problem is that people are obedient while the jails are full of petty thieves . . . the grand thieves are running the country.

—HOWARD ZINN

Howard Zinn, a World War II veteran, member of Veterans for Peace, and professor emeritus at Boston University, was a key figure in opposition to the Vietnam War during the 1960s and a lifelong activist for peace and social justice. He was also a historian and playwright. He authored the controversial book *A People's History of the United States* that showed history through the lens of those who were victimized by events of the past. *A People's History of the United States* was nominated for the American Book Award in 1981, boasting a sales record of more than one million copies.

Zinn was raised in Brooklyn in a working-class neighborhood by immigrant parents. At eighteen, he worked in a shipyard and later flew bomber missions in World War II. His experiences helped form his views about war and his zeal to portray history in a less sanitized manner. Taking advantage of the GI Bill, Zinn went back to school after his military service and worked his way up to a doctor of philosophy in History from Columbia University. Later, he taught at Spelman College in Atlanta, a traditionally Black women's college. There, he got involved in the civil rights movement. When he lent his support to student protestors, the school fired him. His next teaching assignment was as a professor of political science at Boston University where he received tenure and taught until his retirement in 1988. Not one to remain idle, Zinn continued to write and speak across the country. He wrote many books, including his autobiography *You Can't Be Neutral on a Moving Train* and the plays *Marx in Soho* and *Passionate Declarations*. He received the Lannan Foundation Literary Award for Nonfiction and the Eugene V. Debs award for his writing and political activism.

Suggested Reading

Zinn, Howard. *A People's History of the United States*. New York: Harper Perennial, 2015.

———. *Disobedience and Democracy: Nine Fallacies on Law and Order*. Cambridge, MA: South End, 2002.

———. *You Can't Be Neutral on a Moving Train: A Personal History*. Boston: Beacon, 2002.

3

Peacemaking Organizations

THERE ARE MORE PEACEMAKING organizations on our planet than
we could possibly cover in one chapter. Here we have chosen a
small sample representing the diverse and important work being
done by groups devoted to positive peace. We want to call special
attention to the eight veterans organizations that represent a growing number of former service people dedicated to the abolishment
of war. The proliferation of veterans organizations speaks to the
costs of war for those who fight it and demonstrates the many
actions that can be taken to advance conflict transformation and
positive peace.

ALLIANCE FOR PEACEBUILDING (AFP)

Allianceforpeacebuilding.org

The AfP is a nonpartisan network of more than 120 organizations
working in 153 countries to end violent conflict and sustain peace.
Its members include development organizations, academic institutions, and humanitarian and faith-based groups from around the
world. AfP sees its work in terms of coalition building, supporting
"coalitions in key areas of strategy and policy to elevate the entire

peacebuilding field, tackling issues too large for any one organization to address alone."[1] The organization works to be a change agent in the peacebuilding field, fostering innovative strategies to prevent wars and end violence. Its vision "is a world where each person feels secure, dignified, and included, a world where people build peace and manage conflict without violence."[2]

AMERICAN FRIENDS SERVICE COMMITTEE (AFSC)

Afsc.org

The AFSC is an organization that promotes lasting peace with justice as a practical expression of faith in action. Drawing on continuing spiritual insights and working with people of many backgrounds, it sees itself as nurturing the seeds of change and respect for human life that transform social relations and systems. It has nearly a century of experience building peace in communities worldwide. Founded in the crucible of World War I by Quakers who aimed to serve both humanity and country while being faithful to their commitment to nonviolence, AFSC has worked throughout the world in conflict zones, in areas affected by natural disasters, and in oppressed communities to address the root causes of war and violence.

AMNESTY INTERNATIONAL (AI)

Amnesty.org

AI is an NGO global movement of more than three million supporters, members, and activists in over 150 countries and territories who campaign to end grave abuses of human rights. AI's vision is for every person to enjoy all the rights enshrined in the Universal Declaration of Human Rights and other international

1. Alliance for Peacebuilding, "What We Do."
2. Alliance for Peacebuilding, "What We Do."

human rights standards. One of its most effective and famous programs is its letter writing campaign by which AI members around the world send letters of protest to leaders of oppressive governments who have unjustly imprisoned their citizens and letters of support and hope to those imprisoned citizens who have confined their activism to nonviolent actions. Many dissidents have been released by these letter-writing campaigns because the governments keeping their nonviolent citizens in jail don't want the negative publicity.

ARTICLE 9 SOCIETY

Article9society.org

The Article 9 Society, founded by the late Charles Overby, is an international NGO that promotes the protection of article 9 in the Japanese Constitution. This article, which severely restricts Japan's war making powers, was added to the Japanese Constitution after World War II as a condition of Japan's surrender and postwar peace. For nearly seventy years, it has supported Japan's commitment to renounce war as a national right and prohibit the buildup of armed forces. Article 9 is constantly under threat of being abolished from internal sources in Japan as well as external pressures.

BREAKING THE SILENCE

Breakingthesilence.org.il

Breaking the Silence is an organization of veteran combatants who have served in the Israeli military since the start of the Second Intifada and whose mission is to expose the public to the daily realities of Israeli military rule over Palestinian civilian populations. The organization was founded in 2004 by a group of soldiers who served in Hebron. According to their website, "We endeavor to stimulate public debate about the price paid for a reality in which young soldiers face a civilian population on a daily basis, and are engaged in the control of that population's everyday life."[3] The organization seeks to raise awareness of the abuses carried out against civilian populations as well as the cost of participating in these abuses for Israeli servicemen and women. They have collected, researched, and archived more than one thousand testimonies from soldiers representing all strata of Israeli society.

CODEPINK—WOMEN FOR PEACE

Codepink.org

CODEPINK is a feminist, grassroots organization self-described as "a women-initiated grassroots peace and social justice movement working to end US-funded wars and occupations, to challenge militarism globally, and to redirect our resources into health care, education, green jobs, and other life-affirming activities."[4] Founded by Jodie Evans, Medea Benjamin, and Gael Murphy, the organization got its start in November 2002 with a four-month peace vigil at the White House to protest the US-led war in Iraq. Over ten thousand people participated in the vigil. Since then, the organization has developed a worldwide network committed to promoting peace and social justice.

COMBATANTS FOR PEACE

Cfpeace.org

Combatants for Peace (CFP) is a nonviolent, non-profit organization that works to achieve peace between Israel and Palestine. It is composed of former Israeli and Palestinian combat soldiers who have come to the realization that the dispute between Israelis and Palestinians must be settled nonviolently, and that only by joining forces will we be able to end the cycle of violence and bloodshed. CFP uses dialogue and reconciliation strategies to raise public

3. Breaking the Silence, "About."
4. CODEPINK, "What Is CODEPINK?"

consciousness of the shared suffering experienced by both sides of the conflict, to educate people about nonviolent struggle, to pressure governments to end violence and occupation, and to resume constructive dialogue.

COURAGE TO RESIST

Couragetoresist.org

Courage to Resist is a grassroots organization that represents and supports service members who have resisted war and occupation through a myriad of actions—by becoming conscientious objectors, going absent without leave, speaking out against injustice, or refusing to fight. Courage to Resist raises funds, works with the families, and organizes legal representation and public education campaigns. By supporting informed resistance, counter-recruitment, and draft resistance, Courage to Resist hopes to diminish the number of troops available to fight in unjust wars and occupations.

PEACE AND JUSTICE STUDIES ASSOCIATION (PJSA)

Peacejusticestudies.org

PJSA, founded in 2001, is dedicated to bringing together academics, kindergarten through twelfth grade teachers, and grassroots activists to explore alternatives to violence and share visions and strategies for peacebuilding, social justice, and social change. PJSA also serves as a professional association for scholars in the field of peace and conflict resolution studies, and is the North American affiliate of the International Peace Research Association. PJSA has members worldwide, but mainly in Canada and the US. It publishes a regular newsletter ("The Peace Chronicle"), maintains a member network and LISTSERV, publishes the *Global Directory of Peace Studies and Conflict Resolution Programs*, and offers a speakers' bureau.

GLOBAL ACTION TO PREVENT WAR

Gapwblog.wordpress.com

Founded in 1999, Global Action to Prevent War describes itself as a "transnational network of organizations dedicated to ending armed violence and severe human rights violations through policy analysis and collaborative action."[5] Global Action has a goal of peace and human security in a phased, integrated step-by-step program over several decades in the areas of conflict prevention, nuclear and conventional disarmament, and building a culture of peace.

GOLD STAR FAMILIES FOR PEACE (GSFP)

GSFP is a non-profit US-based organization founded in 2005 to protest US military action in Iraq and to support people who lost a member of their family while performing active military service in Iraq. GSFP was founded by Cindy Sheehan whose son, Casey, was killed in Iraq in 2004. The organization has participated in a large number of anti-war events in collaboration with Veterans for Peace, United for Peace and Justice, CODEPINK, Military Families Speak Out, and others. It provides an alternative to Gold Star Mothers, an organization that is made up of mothers who lost children in war but does not have a vocal anti-war agenda.

GREENPEACE

Greenpeace.org

Greenpeace is an independent global organization that works to change thinking, to protect and conserve the environment, and to promote peace. Its programmatic goals include revolutionizing the planet's energy use, defending oceans, conserving forests, advancing disarmament, countering the use of toxic chemicals, and

5. Global Action, "About."

promoting sustainable agriculture. Greenpeace was organized in 1971 and is present today in countries across Europe, North America, South America, Asia, Africa, and the Pacific.

HAGUE APPEAL FOR PEACE

Creducation.net/intl-orgs/the-hague-appeal-for-peace/

The Hague Appeal for Peace is an international network of organizations and individuals dedicated to the abolition of war and making peace a human right. The Global Campaign for Peace Education was launched at the Hague Appeal for Peace conference in May 1999, which met to celebrate the one hundredth anniversary of the 1899 Hague Peace Conference. The centennial conference was attended by ten thousand peace advocates across the globe, including Dr. Leo Sandy. After the conference, the Hague Appeal for Peace took the responsibility of coordinating a campaign dedicated to supporting peace through the collection of stories of peace work around the world.

MILITARY FAMILIES SPEAK OUT (MFSO)

Militaryfamiliesspeakout.com

MFSO is an organization of military families in the US and across the world who have a loved one who has served in the military since 9/11. The organization seeks to oppose unjust military interventions and support veterans upon their return home. MFSO opposes the deployment of troops or use of military force unless as a last resort in order to defend against a direct danger.

PAX CHRISTI INTERNATIONAL

Paxchristi.net

Pax Christi International is a global Catholic peace movement and network that works to help establish peace, respect for human rights, justice, and reconciliation in areas of the world that are torn by conflict. It is grounded in the belief that peace is possible and that vicious cycles of violence and injustice can be broken. It aims to coordinate and represent the global peace movement at the international policy level, prioritizing space for local voices and partnerships. Pax Christi International's advocacy priorities include just peace in Israel and Palestine, nuclear weapons and disarmament, and ecological justice. The organization holds special consultative status with the UN.

PEACE ACTION

Peaceaction.org

Peace Action is the largest grassroots peace organization in the US, with chapters in many states across the country. The organization has been working for a world without war and violence for a half century. An important part of their activity, apart from public peace education, is to help shape US foreign policy away from militarism and towards more international cooperation. Their mission is a world of peace in which the menace of nuclear weapons has forever been erased from our planet, war has been abolished as a method of solving conflicts, and all human beings can live in health and dignity and participate in making decisions that advance the common good.

PEACE BRIGADES INTERNATIONAL (PBI)

Peacebrigades.org

PBI is a global NGO that has worked to protect human rights through the discipline of nonviolence since 1981. Their main idea was to form an organization of trained volunteers to undertake nonviolent third party intervention to foster peacemaking, avoid the outbreak of violence, and protect human rights in situations of high tension. This is sometimes called the principle of "protective accompaniment." One of their earliest interventions was in Nicaragua in 1983 near the Honduran border. Ten PBI volunteers interposed themselves between US-backed Contras and Sandanista forces to help prevent hostilities.

PUGWASH CONFERENCES ON SCIENCE AND WORLD AFFAIRS

Pugwash.org

Pugwash Conferences is a transnational NGO that aims to advance a world free of nuclear weapons and weapons of mass destruction through dialogue and the support of scientific, evidence-based policymaking. Pugwash was formed in 1957 with the idea that scientists on both sides of the Iron Curtain who understood the dangers of nuclear war should meet to share ideas on how to avoid nuclear holocaust and to help promote arms control in their respective countries. The organization was initially inspired by the Russell–Einstein Manifesto (1955), which called for new thinking for the abolition of nuclear weapons and war. Pugwash scientists in both the US and the Soviet Union worked together behind the scenes to help bring about arms control treaties and an end to the Cold War. Pugwash (and its founder, Joseph Rotblat) received the Nobel Peace Prize in 1995.

VETERANS AGAINST NUCLEAR ARMS (VANA)

VANA was founded in Halifax, Nova Scotia, Canada in 1982 under the name of Veterans for Multilateral Nuclear Disarmament and later changed its name in 1986. Its mission included working for the abolishment of war and nuclear weapons, supporting the UN and UN peacekeeping operations, achieving global common security through international law, and joining with veterans worldwide to end arms races.

VIETNAM VETERANS AGAINST THE WAR (VVAW)

Vvaw.org

VVAW is a national veterans' organization founded in New York in 1967 following a peace demonstration by six Vietnam veterans. VVAW voiced growing opposition among returning servicemen and women to the war in Southeast Asia and grew to over thirty thousand members in the US and in Vietnam. The organization used grassroots action to protest the unjust nature of the war. They assisted returning veterans with counseling and physical therapy and worked to create job programs to help veterans reintegrate into society. VVAW argues that true patriotism requires opposition to unjust military ventures, the advancement of peace and social and economic justice for all people, and dignity and respect for veterans.

VETERANS FOR PEACE, INC. (VFP)

Veteransforpeace.org

VFP is a global organization of military veterans and allies building a culture of peace through experience and advocacy. They work to inform the public about the causes and costs of war. With over 140 chapters worldwide, VFP pledges to use nonviolent means to maintain a democratic and inclusive organization working for world peace. VFP's specific goals include restraining governments from intervening in the internal affairs of other nations, ending arms races and nuclear weapons, seeking justice for veterans and victims of war, and abolishing war as an instrument of national policy.[6]

WORLD BEYOND WAR (WBW)

Worldbeyondwar.org

WBWar defines itself as a global nonviolent movement to end war and establish a just and sustainable peace. Founded in 2014 by David Hartsough and David Swanson, WBW aims to foster popular support for ending war, advance the abolishment of war as an institution, and replace a culture of war with a culture of peace. The organization works through peace education, nonviolent direct action, and media.[7]

6. Veterans for Peace, "Who We Are."
7. World Beyond War, "About."

4

Peace Studies Programs and Journals

Several decades ago there were a handful of peace and social justices programs, but their numbers have grown exponentially and continue to grow, with programs for certificates, undergraduate majors, and master of arts and doctorate degrees. Currently, there are more than 450 peace and social justice programs around the world. As the study of peace and social justice has grown, so too have the number of peace-related academic journals. This chapter is intended to be a resource for students exploring peace-related educational opportunities and publications. It is not exhaustive, but merely a sample of the rich field that has developed.

THE GLOBAL DIRECTORY OF PEACE STUDIES AND CONFLICT RESOLUTION PROGRAMS

Peacejusticestudies.org/school-directory/

This global directory is a comprehensive, annotated guide to peace studies and conflict resolution programs at colleges and universities worldwide. Here we provide the link to its most current edition, which profiles undergraduate and postgraduate programs in forty countries and thirty-eight US states.

THE PEACE AND JUSTICE STUDIES ASSOCIATION

Peacejusticestudies.org/journals

The Peace and Justice Studies Association website hosts a list of many publications in the field of peace studies. We have highlighted a few of those publications below and included bulletins and online newsletters related to specific topics such as nuclear disarmament.

BULLETIN OF THE ATOMIC SCIENTISTS

Thebulletin.org

Established in 1945, the Bulletin of Atomic Scientists aims to make policymakers and global audiences aware of the threats caused by nuclear weapons, climate change, and emerging technologies to human survival and development. It publishes information from scientists and security experts who explore the dangers of human-made technologies, fostering conversation between academics, scientists, and the public. In 2007, the Bulletin received the National Magazine Award for General Excellence for translating the technical and esoteric language of nuclear weapons policy and international security into engaging and readable formats. The Bulletin supports fellowships and awards for students and young journalists.

INTERNATIONAL JOURNAL OF PEACE STUDIES

Jstor.org/journal/intejpeacstud

The *International Journal of Peace Studies* is published twice every year by the International Peace Research Association. The journal is dedicated to promoting dialogue on a range of issues in peace research, including human security, peace and war, environmental movements, economic equity, conflict resolution, disarmament, and peace education.

PEACE & CHANGE: A JOURNAL OF PEACE RESEARCH

Onlinelibrary.wiley.com/journal/14680130

Peace & Change is an international and multidisciplinary journal dedicated to advancing global peace, justice, and inclusivity. The journal aims to bridge the gap between researchers, practitioners, activists, and educators working in peace and related issues such as conflict transformation, nonviolence, economic development, race and gender studies, and more.

PEACE REVIEW: A JOURNAL OF SOCIAL JUSTICE

Tandfonline.com/loi/cper20

Peace Review is a quarterly, multidisciplinary, and transnational journal that publishes on current issues related to the promotion of a more peaceful world. The journal defines peace research broadly and accepts pieces on topics that include peace, human rights, ecology, development, and culture.

THE ACORN: PHILOSOPHICAL STUDIES IN PACIFISM AND NONVIOLENCE

Acornjournal.net/

Published biannually, *The Acorn* is a peer-reviewed, academic journal devoted to the philosophical examination of the theory and practice of activism, nonviolence, organizing, pacifism, protest, people-power, and resistance especially as relates to examples such as Mahatma Gandhi, Martin Luther King Jr., Cesar Chavez, or Jane Addams. The journal was established in 1986 by Ha Poong Kim.

5

World Religions and Peace

We have just enough religion to make us hate but
not enough to make us love one another.

—Jonathan Swift

Religion has played a major role in both war and peace. Nearly
every prominent religion of the world has given rise to individuals
who use their interpretation of their faith to justify horrendous
forms of discrimination and violence. Thus, it was possible for Hitler to write in *Mein Kampf*, "Hence today I believe that I am acting
in accordance with the will of the Almighty Creator: by defending
myself against the Jew, I am fighting for the work of the Lord."[1]
More recently, extremist Buddhist monks in Myanmar have in-
cited violence against the country's Muslims and non-Buddhist
minorities, citing the need to protect Buddhism from foreign religions.[2] In 2013, a local newspaper captured scenes shockingly at
odds with a religion devoted to nonviolence:

> Buddhist monks armed with swords and machetes Friday
> stalked the streets of a city in central Myanmar, where

1. Hitler, *Mein Kampf*, 60.
2. Greene, "You Will Have."

sectarian violence that has left about 20 people dead has
begun to spread to other areas. . . . A group of about one
hundred Buddhists, including some monks, went around
Meiktila on Thursday night torching mosques.[3]

Within religions, violent confrontation can emerge between sects, as it has between Sunni and Shiite Muslims. Christianity also has a long and bloody history of being used to mobilize violence against those considered enemies of the faith, both external and internal. And yet, the great peacemakers of the world include many people of faith for whom religion is a source of inspiration and strength. Religious peacemakers may even owe their persistence in the face of diversity to their religious beliefs and scriptures because suffering is seen as a form of redemption.

Religion has been a source of violence and peace in the world and will likely continue to be until human development is advanced to a point where people are better able to see their own humanity in others. High quality education and effective parenting are important contributors to such an outcome, and economic and social justice worldwide have much to do with lowering tensions by having people's basic needs met. Oppression, poverty, and violence undermine human development and make it possible for religion to be used for destructive purposes.

Many who subscribe to the major religions of the world would be surprised to learn of the commonalities their faiths share, including placing a high value on peace and nonviolence. We chose to include a brief discussion of the religions below because we wanted readers to understand some of the basic aspects of these major religions and their potential for moving the world toward the abolition of war and the establishment of social and economic justice.

3. Wai Lin, "Armed Buddhists."

Suggested Reading

Center for Interreligious Understanding. "Uniting the World's Religions for Peace." https://www.ciunow.org/insights/vatican-conference-seeks-peace/.

Smock, David R., ed. *Religious Contributions to Peacemaking: When Religion Brings Peace, Not War*. Washington, DC: United States Institute of Peace, 2006. https://www.files.ethz.ch/isn/29931/2006_january_pw55.pdf

BUDDHISM

Better than a thousand hollow words is one word that brings peace.

—THE BUDDHA

An estimated five hundred million people, roughly 7 percent of the world's population, practice Buddhism. The religion's name originates from *budhi* ("to awaken"). It had its beginnings 2,500 years ago when Siddhartha Gautama, wandering religious teacher commonly referred to as the Buddha, awakened at the age of thirty-five. Around the age of twenty-nine, Gautama, who was born into a royal family in Lumbini, now located in Nepal, became aware that wealth and luxury did not guarantee happiness. He studied religion and philosophy for several years until he became enlightened. From then until his death at the age of eighty, he taught the precepts of Buddhism called the Dhamma ("Truth").

Buddhism focuses on compassion and the connection of all things to each other, emphasizing nonviolence, personal enlightenment, meditation, loving kindness, and social responsibility. As Gordon and Grob note,

> Buddhism teaches that we are the author of our own future, both as individuals and as creative members of society. It is thus within our power to create the world in which we live. It can be a world at peace or a world in ruins. The choice is ours.[4]

---

4. Gordon and Grob, *Education for Peace*, 122.

The basic requirements of Buddhism are not to do evil, to cultivate good, and to purify one's mind. The five precepts of Buddhism, which serve as the foundational ethical code for Buddhists, instruct followers to abstain from harming living beings, stealing, sexual misconduct, lying, and intoxication. The ten meritorious deeds, known as the Ten Punna Kiriya Vatthu, are: charity, morality, mental cultivation, reverence, service, sharing merits, rejoicing in the merits of others, preaching the Dhamma (the teachings of Buddha), listening to the Dhamma, and correcting one's views.

Traditionally, Buddhism has been a contemplative and mindful religion. Buddhist monks are considered above politics and are often cloistered with little contact with the outside world. A new movement within Buddhism called "engaged Buddhism," inspired by Buddhist monk Thich Nhat Hanh, requires that monks be a part of their communities by serving them and engaging in efforts to promote world peace and social justice. This movement is similar to Catholic liberation theology, which developed in Central America in the 1970s.

CHRISTIANITY

And the fruit of righteousness is sown in
peace of them that make peace.

—JAMES 3:18, KJV

The world's largest religion is based on the teachings of Jesus of Nazareth. Christians believe that Jesus was the incarnation of God who came to earth to reveal God's love for humanity through his life, death, and resurrection as proclaimed in the Bible's four Gospels. Salvation for Christians is faith in Jesus, which is eternal life in God's kingdom. After the Romans crucified Jesus, his apostles spread his teachings. The religion suffered more than a century of Roman persecution due in large part to the pacifistic beliefs of adherents. After the religious conversion of Emperor Constantine (312 CE), Christianity became the official religion of the Roman

Empire (380 CE). This unification of church and state contributed significantly to participation in war by Christians and the erosion of Christian pacifism and martyrdom.

The Christian Church experienced several splits in the ensuing centuries and is now represented by several different denominations, including the Roman Catholic Church, the Eastern Orthodox Church, and Protestant denominations. While they differ in their use of symbolism and liturgy and in their interpretations of the Bible, they all share central doctrines based on the teachings of Jesus and his life, death, and resurrection as found in the New Testament.

The Old Testament book of Isaiah refers to Jesus Christ as the "Prince of Peace" (Isa 9:6). Jesus's message in the New Testament is one of compassion, love, forgiveness, generosity, service, and nonviolence. In fact, Christianity was completely nonviolent until it became the state religion of Rome; its guiding principles of nonviolence were later redefined by the doctrine of just war, which dates to St. Augustine (354–430). The following quotes emphasize the biblical basis of the theme of peace:

- "But my steadfast love shall not depart from you, and my covenant of peace shall not be removed, says the LORD, who has compassion on you" (Isa 54:10 ESV).

- The Gospel of Luke records Jesus weeping over Jerusalem and its people who expected a messiah to militarily overthrow the Romans; but Jesus says, "If you, even you, had only recognized on this day the things that make for peace" (Luke 19:42 NRSV).

- Even Jesus's crucifixion, a violent act of capital punishment in the Roman Empire, is understood by Christians through the resurrection of Jesus as ending hostility among peoples. On the cross, Jesus called for forgiveness rather than revenge. Ephesians aptly interprets the meaning of Jesus's death and resurrection: "that he might create in himself one new humanity in place of the two, thus making peace, and might reconcile both groups to God in one body through the cross, thus putting to death hostility through it. So he came and proclaimed peace to you who were far off and peace to those who were near" (Eph 2:15–17 NRSV).

Jesus himself taught about the virtues of peace, forgiveness, and love:

- "Blessed are the peacemakers, for they shall be called the children of God" (Matt 5:9 NIV).

- "You have heard that it was said, 'An eye for an eye and a tooth for a tooth'. But I say to you, Do not resist the one who is evil. But if anyone slaps you on the right cheek, turn to them the other also" (Matt 5:38–39 ESV).

- "Love your enemies, do good to those who hate you, bless those who curse you, pray for those who abuse you" (Luke 6:27–28 ESV).

- "A new commandment I give to you, that you love one another; as I have loved you, that you also love one another" (John 13:34 NKJV).

Christians are not monolithic in their theological interpretations. Throughout the centuries they have had various responses, rightly and wrongly, to Jesus's question "Who do you say I am?"[5] However, Christians need to carefully study the Scriptures before using the Christian faith to justify acts of violence. Jesus calls his followers to peace.

HINDUISM

A spiritually illumined soul lives in the world,
yet is never contaminated by it.

—SWAMI BHASKARANANDA

---

5. For example, see Luke 9:20.

Hinduism is amongst the oldest of the world religions, originating in the Indus Valley around 3000 to 2000 BCE. Today, it is practiced by close to 80 percent of people in India. The term "Hinduism" encapsulates the rich and diverse array of beliefs and practices that have grown from a common root of the Vedas, which developed about the mid-second millennium BCE. The earliest Veda is predominantly evocations, prayers, and sacrifices to powerful natural deities such as the Sun, Fire, and Wind. Gradually in the later Vedic period there developed sophisticated philosophic ideas in the Upanishads. One of the key ideas in the Upanishads is the search for knowledge to help people escape from the cycle of rebirth (reincarnation). Hinduism came about from the Vedic religion of ancient India. The major branches of Hinduism include Vaishnavism and Shaivism, each of which includes many different sects. Each sect relies on its own set of scriptures, but all revere the ancient Vedas.

An essential element of Hinduism is the belief in a cosmic principle of ultimate reality called *brahman* and its common identity with an individual's essence, or *atman*. All humans and animals go through cycles of rebirth, or *samsara*, which can be ended only by spiritual self-realization, after which liberation, or *moksha*, is attained. The principle of *karma*, both cause and effect, determines a being's status within the cycle of rebirth. The Hindu deities that have the largest following are Vishnu and Shiva, who are worshipped in various avatars, or incarnations.

The goddess Durga also has a large following. The major sources of classical stories about dharma are the Mahabharata, which includes the Bhagavadgita (one of the most important religious texts of Hinduism), the Ramayana, and the Puranas. There is no central authority or church-like organization that holds Hinduism together. It has a continuous tradition of spiritual adepts and teachers called gurus who realize, reinterpret, and teach the dharma. The hierarchical social structure of the caste system has traditionally been practiced in Hinduism but not without serious challenge by figures like Gandhi; the system is also banned by the Indian Constitution. Hinduism should not be misconstrued for

"Hindutva"—a political ideology of Hindu nationalism that has become a potent political force in Indian politics.

Hinduism is synonymous with nonviolence with its antipathy toward *himsa* or violence, but it was not always that way. War and capital punishment were allowed under the Vedic traditions. As the ascetic non-vedic belief systems gained in ascendancy due to the rise of Jainism and Buddhism and more recently in Gandhi's nonviolent movement, Hinduism moved more toward a strict or ascetic interpretation of nonviolence. Thus, it eschewed any violence against people, animals, and even plants. What evolved was a strongly held belief that "all violence is rooted in ignorance (*avidya*) and all nonviolence in knowledge."[6] A basic tenet of Hinduism is a reverence for life. "Killing animals for pleasure and profit, destroying rivers and forests, and polluting the atmosphere and the interior of the earth are harmful to living beings and will eventually result in the destruction of humankind itself."[7] In addition to its core element of nonviolence, Hinduism also stresses ideals such as truthfulness, celibacy, friendship, compassion, fortitude, self-control, purity, cleanliness, contentment, prayers, austerity, perseverance, penance, pious company, and generosity.

ISLAM

The taking of one innocent life is like taking all of Mankind
. . . and the saving of one life is like saving all of Mankind.

—QUR'AN 5:33

"Islam" literally means submission. But the root is the same as that of the word for peace—"*salaam*." The most recent of the three great monotheistic religions (the other two are Judaism and Christianity), Islam was founded by Prophet Muhammad in the seventh century. Other Islamic prophets include Abraham and Jesus, although in the Islamic tradition Jesus is not recognized as the divine Son

6. Gordon and Grob, *Education for Peace*, 141.
7. Gordon and Grob, *Education for Peace*, 144.

of God, but as a great prophet who will return at the end of the world as the Messiah to convert Jews and Christians to Islam and to help the Mahdi (the spiritual leader) preside over a perfected Islamic world. Although Jews and Christians are believed to have wrongly interpreted the great prophets, they are considered "people of the book"; they worship the same God (Allah) as Muslims and warrant respect. The main sources of Islamic doctrine come from the Qur'an (the holy book dictated by Allah to Muhammad) and the Sunnah (the way of the Prophet, as expressed in his deeds and words). Both are of highest importance in determining man-made law (*sharia*), which has evolved over time and varies among Muslim states. The five pillars, or core practices, of Islam are the declaration of faith (*shahada*), prayer (*salah*), almsgiving (*zakat*), fasting during the month of Ramadan (*sawm*), and the pilgrimage to Mecca (*Hajj*).

Former US president George W. Bush once characterized Islam as a religion of peace.[8] Historically, like many religions that gained popular support and political power, Islam has engaged in holy wars and some of its members have practiced religious intolerance to the chagrin of its spiritual adherents; this has included violent disputes between Sunni and Shiite Muslims, who split over disagreements over leadership succession after Muhammad's death. As in Christianity, however, if we look at the religion's ideals we find among its fundamental virtues faith, love, charity, mercy, compassion, and forgiveness.

Practicing peace in one's life is considered essential for Muslims. One Muslim out of many who became widely known for his practice of nonviolence was Abdul Gaffar Khan, a member of the often warlike Pathans on the northwest frontier of India, who was influenced by Gandhi in leading his people to independence through the establishment of Pakistan. Another significant figure in Islam is Muhammad Ali Jinnah, the founder of Pakistan, who worked closely with Gandhi to oust the British from India. Besides being a lawyer and politician,he was the leader of the All-India Muslim League and Pakistan's first governor-general. He is revered

8. White House, "'Islam Is Peace.'"

as *Quaid-i-Azam* (great leader) and *Baba-i-Qaum* (father of the nation). He believed strongly that Indian Muslims should have their own state. Hence, Pakistan was established due mostly to his efforts.

The following are examples of passages from the Qur'an and Hadith (sayings of the Prophet) that support Islamic hopes for peace:

- "There shall be no compulsion in religion" (Qur'an 2:256).

- "The (true) servants of (God), the Most Gracious, are those who walk on the earth in humility, and when the ignorant address them, reply with (words of) peace" (Qur'an 25:63).

- "Fight for the sake of Allah those who fight against you, but do not attack them first. Allah does not love aggressors" (Qur'an 2:190).

- "God has revealed to me that you should adopt humility so that no one oppresses another."[9]

- "The best fighting . . . is (to speak) a word of justice to an oppressive ruler."[10]

JUDAISM

What is hurtful to yourself do not do to your fellow man. That is the whole of the Torah and the remainder is but commentary.

—TALMUD, SHABBAT 31A

Judaism dates back almost four thousand years, beginning in the ancient Near Eastern region of Canaan where Israel and Palestine are now located. Judaism traces its heritage to the covenant God made with Abraham and his lineage—that God would make them a sacred people and give them a holy land. The primary figures of

9. an-Nawawi, *Riyad as-Salihin*, 1589.
10. as-Sijistani, *Sunan Abi Dawud*, 4344.

Israelite culture include the patriarchs Abraham, Isaac, Jacob, and the prophet Moses who received God's law and commandments at Mount Sinai. Judaism is a tradition grounded in the religious, ethical, and social laws as they are articulated in the Torah—the first five books of the Hebrew Bible. Jews refer to the Bible as the Tanakh, an acronym for the texts of the Torah, Prophets, and Writings. Other sacred texts include the Talmud and Midrash, the rabbinic, legal, and narrative interpretations of the Torah. Contemporary branches of Judaism differ in their interpretations and applications of these texts. The four main movements within Judaism today are Orthodox, Conservative, Reform, and Reconstructionist, respectively ranging from traditional to liberal to religiously progressive in their application of Torah.

While diverse in their views, Jews are unified based on their common connection to a set of sacred narratives expressing their relationship with God as a holy people. Judaism tends to emphasize practice over belief. Jewish worship is centered in synagogues, which replaced the Second Temple after its destruction in 70 CE. Jewish religious leaders, who oversee the many rituals and ceremonies essential to Jewish religious practice, are called rabbis.

Judaism has a long history in the promotion of peace and social justice. For example, a major mantra and inspiration of the worldwide peace movement has its origins in Judaism: "They shall beat their swords into plowshares, and their spears into pruning hooks; nation shall not lift up sword against nation, neither shall they learn war anymore" (Isa 2:2–4). Also, in the rabbinic tradition as stated in Sanhedrin 37a: "Therefore one man was created . . . to teach you that he who kills one soul, of him it is said that it is as if he had killed an entire world for he destroys all that would have come from that one person, and he who saves the life of one person, of him it is as if he had saved an entire world."[11] This compares nicely to a passage from the Qur'an: "The taking of one innocent life is like taking all of Mankind . . . and the saving of one life is like saving all of Mankind" (5:33). Gordon and Grob point out that *shalom* "derives from a Hebrew root meaning 'wholeness' or

11. Gordon and Grob, *Education for Peace*, 34.

'completeness,' the state of positive well-being that . . . is our task as God's workers to help realize."[12] *Tikkun Olam*, which translates to "world repair," is also a phrase that highlights the peaceful nature of Judaism. It is commonly used to refer to the pursuit of social action and social justice. It is clear that Judaism, like other major religions, has a mandate to seek peace and justice in the world, and it calls on all of us to make strong efforts in that endeavor.

Suggested Reading

Anjum, Muhammed R. "Concept of Peace in World's Major Religions: An Analysis." *International Journal of Scientific and Research Publications* 7 (2017) 248–59.

Chinmoy, Sri. "World Peace from a Hindu Perspective: A Hindu World-Peace-Dreamer." Sri Chinmoy Library. https://www.srichinmoylibrary.com/pcp-3.

Fahey, Joseph. *War and the Christian Conscience: Where Do You Stand?* Maryknoll, NY: Orbis, 2005.

Israel & Judaism Studies. "The Ideal of Peace in Judaism." https://ijs.org.au/the-ideal-of-peace-in-judaism/.

Malkin, John. "In Engaged Buddhism, Peace Begins with You." Lion's Roar, July 1, 2003. https://www.lionsroar.com/in-engaged-buddhism-peace-begins-with-you/.

Omar, Manal. "Islam Is a Religion of Peace. *Foreign Policy*. Nov. 9, 2015. https://foreignpolicy.com/2015/11/09/islam-is-a-religion-of-peace-manal-omar-debate-islamic-state/.

12. Gordon and Grob, *Education for Peace*, 42.

6

Make Peace:
Suggestions for Citizen Projects

Never doubt that a small group of thoughtful, committed citizens
can change the world; indeed, it's the only thing that ever has.

—MARGARET MEAD

VIOLENCE AND WAR CAN have no part in bringing about a genuinely peaceful world. Genuine peace must be brought about *without* war by nonviolent (and preferably legal) means. Below we offer
steps that we believe would promote a more peaceful world without
the use of violence. The authors are writing from the US and some
of the ideas offered here reflect that vantage point. We encourage
readers to add their own ideas to this list that leverage and respond
to the unique opportunities that exist in their own nations.

DEMOCRATIZATION OF THE UN

The United Nations is our one great hope for a peaceful and free world.

—RALPH BUNCHE

As we noted in chapter 1, the UN Security Council—which has authority under the UN Charter to maintain international peace, including the marshalling of military force from member states if necessary—has serious weaknesses. For one, the fifteen-member Council's majority vote can be, and often has been, blocked by the veto power of any one of its five permanent members (the so-called "big five")—the US, UK, Russia, France, and China. This violates the democratic principle of majority rule and has protected the national interests of the permanent five and their allies at the expense of international law.

Replacing the veto privilege with a large majority requirement would remove a barrier to world justice and the even application of international law. While it would not solve all the democratic shortcomings of the UN, it seems to us a step in the right direction. There is a democratic issue with the General Assembly as well; each member nation gets the same number of votes regardless of the size of its citizenry. Thus, the Republic of the Marshall Islands with a population of under forty thousand gets the same representative weight as India with a population of more than one billion. We leave it to your constructive imaginations to suggest a fix (remember, the first step in remedying a wrong is to make it known to the public conscience).

DISARMAMENT: OBLIGATIONS TO MEET

Disarmament or limitation of armaments, which depends on the progress made on security, also contributes to the maintenance of peace.

—LUDWIG QUIDDE

Contrary to what one might suppose, general and complete disarmament is something to which most nations are legally committed already (see article 6 of the Nuclear Nonproliferation Treaty). The US and the Soviet Union even agreed in 1961 on the steps to achieve this aim in the McCloy–Zorin Agreement. Some disarmament—involving both nuclear and conventional weapons—between the

Cold War superpowers has already taken place since the end of the Cold War. Organization like Global Zero have gained considerable international support for a plan to abolish nuclear weapons by 2030. Former secretary of defense Chuck Hagel endorsed Global Zero in 2010, and President Barak Obama publicly embraced the idea of total nuclear disarmament in his first year in office in 2008.

So how do we advance the process of disarmament? By reminding our lawmakers and leaders of our long standing, and long overdue, legal obligation to do it. This message can be sent to our government representatives and to our local newspaper editors. It also can and should be raised as a reminder to our national electoral candidates at their Q&A sessions in forthcoming campaigns. Why not join a peace group in your area and make it a collective project? Remember, the goal for the near term—as the courageous Republic of the Marshall Islands reminded the world in their 2014 lawsuit against the nuclear nine—is not disarmament; it's to start negotiations on disarmament per our obligations under the Nuclear Nonproliferation Treaty.

ARMS TRADE: EMBRACE THE NEW TREATY

Every gun that is made, every warship launched, every rocket fired signifies, in the final sense, a theft from those who hunger and are not fed, those who are cold and are not clothed. The world in arms is not spending money alone. It is spending the sweat of its laborers, the genius of its scientists, the hopes of its children. . . . This is not a way of life at all, in any true sense. Under the cloud of threatening war, it is humanity hanging from a cross of iron.

—DWIGHT D. EISENHOWER

Let's bring the global arms trade under control. This should be undertaken along with negotiations to disarm. Sadly, the main merchants of death are the permanent members of the UN Security Council, and the US is, and has been since the end of the

Cold War, by far the biggest seller of weapons. The arms trade, which amounts to roughly $140 billion each year, is often justified by the sellers as necessary for friendly nations to defend themselves against aggressive neighbors or rebellious internal groups. But even a non-aggressive neighbor who deploys large quantities of weapons in self-defense can *seem* to be planning aggression, increasing the chances that a neighboring state will also amass more weapons. In short, arms trade leads to arms races and, not infrequently, to war. Moreover, armaments frequently end up in black markets abroad and in the possession of violent non-state actors including terrorist groups and gangs.

Tragically, countries like the US have often sold weapons to countries with appalling human rights records. After many defeats in the US Congress, a bill forbidding such sales known as the Arms Trade Code of Conduct passed in 1999. It required the US president to begin negotiations on a treaty on international arms trade. The Arms Trade Treaty (ATT) was overwhelmingly approved by the UN General Assembly in 2013 by a vote of 153–3 with twenty-three abstentions. The treaty has been signed by 130 nations. The US signed but did not ratify the ATT, and in 2019 it emphasized that it was not a party to the treaty. The good news is that the treaty has already met and exceeded the required number of ratifications (fifty) and came into force in international law on December 24, 2014. Citizens can encourage their country to ratify the ATT if they haven't already. Wouldn't it be great if the leading arms merchants of the world were all on board? Let's do it!

THE INTERNATIONAL WEALTH-POVERTY GAP: LET'S CLOSE IT.

Poverty is the worst form of violence.

—MAHATMA GANDHI

It's not hard to see that the problem is really one of spreading the world's wealth around more equitably. This can be done partly through a system whereby UN member states meet the UN goal in which each spends 0.7 percent of its Gross National Income (GNI) on international aid. This alone would increase foreign aid by more than $100 billion a year. Other needed improvements for closing the gap are fairer systems of trade and finance. Both systems currently favor the rich over the poor, and often exploit impoverished and indigenous communities. Developing countries need access to world markets and opportunities for local entrepreneurship. The international system of finance, especially the World Bank and the International Monetary Fund, largely run by and for wealthy nations, should be more understanding and forgiving of the crippling debt burden carried by most of the developing countries, particularly when caused by structural adjustment programs that often destabilize local economies.

Two specific ideas for the development of international revenue to contribute to development plans are the Tobin tax and a tax on military spending. The Tobin tax was originally suggested by Nobel Memorial winning economist James Tobin in 1972. He proposed a tiny tax of 0.5 percent on international financial transactions (such as currency exchanges). Such a tax could easily raise several hundred billion dollars—many times more than current total UN spending. The idea is favored among some EU nations but opposed by the UK and US. Similarly, an international tax on military spending could not only raise tens of billions for much needed non-military purposes, but it could also discourage wasteful spending on armaments. World military spending reached more than $2.4 trillion in 2023.

INCLUDE INTERNATIONAL CIVICS IN SCHOOL CURRICULA

Peace is not merely the absence of war but the presence of justice, of law, of order—in short, of government.

—ALBERT EINSTEIN

The value of civics has long been recognized in education—not just in the US where it is mandated by law in thirty-eight states but in virtually all countries. Yet some schools are reducing or eliminating civics as a subject. Civics has traditionally focused on the nature and workings of government at the local, state, and national levels. An understanding of civics is crucial for good citizenship, and hence, for good government. Can the understanding of the nature and workings of the governing of relations among the nations of the world be any less important? We think not, and we suggest, as a required part of every citizen's education, what might be called "international civics." Its subject matter would focus mainly on the UN—its nature and workings, the ways its functions have served the interests of peace, and the ways in which it could be made more effective in meeting global challenges. Some public school civics curricula do include a unit on international relations, but not many; even fewer examine the history, structure, and functions of the UN. This needs to be changed. And we can start by making the case with our own local schools.

INCLUDE PEACE, SOCIAL JUSTICE, AND CONFLICT RESOLUTION IN SCHOOL CURRICULA

If we are to teach real peace in this world, and if we are to carry on a real war against war, we shall have to begin with the children.

—MAHATMA GANDHI

School history books are full of past battles and war heroes with little mention of peace, social justice, nonviolence, and peace heroes. This leads students to develop values and perspectives that are inimical to peace and social justice, and to judge current peace activists as troublemakers and disrupters of social order. Students should be inspired by those who believed in what could be rather than what is or what was. With exceptions like Howard Zinn's *A People's History of the United States*, history books are written by the winners of wars and rarely show the side of the conquered or oppressed. Violence is typically presented to students as the primary means of solving international disputes, yet a 2011 study done by Chenoweth and Stephan showed that nonviolent resistance has achieved greater gains overall.[1] Unless students are given the full range of information, they are likely to come down on the side of war and violence as ways to resolve conflict.

One promising curricular innovation is service learning, which ties what is being taught in classes directly to a volunteer field experience that offers assistance to schools and agencies in exchange for a high impact and hands-on learning experience that illuminates subjects that relate to the service-learning experience. Since students are placed in sites where various human activities are going on, they can critically examine how those settings promote or hinder human development. They identify what works and what doesn't by comparing what they see to best practices learned in class. This produces awareness that is the necessary step for social action aimed at ameliorating conditions that undermine the health and wellness of people.

Social justice involves civil and human rights. The Universal Declaration of Human Rights should be posted in every school and discussed on a regular basis as part of social studies. Many projects can be generated from this document that would allow students to delve further into what constitutes social justice as well as what they can do to promote it on local, regional, national, and international levels. Youth have three things that make them ideal peacemakers: they can think abstractly; they have high levels of

1. Chenoweth and Stephan, *Why Civil Resistance Works.*

energy; and they are idealistic. With lofty goals in mind and the wherewithal to achieve approximations of them, our youth would be much less inclined to abuse substances, join gangs, drop out of school, commit crimes, and spend hours on social media and video games. Our youth need reasons for being, and we sell them short when we don't provide them. The energy of our youth is being wasted on frivolity and self-destruction instead of being used to solve some of society's most vexing problems. If we invite them, they will come.

Many students lack social and problem-solving skills because of their increasing use of technology and the failure of schools to teach social and conflict resolution skills. School officials often talk about teaching the "whole child" but most aim at the head, and much of what students learn focuses mainly on memorization. Students are made up of a mind, heart, and body, and if they are to be taught holistically, then schools need to help them become people who can think critically for themselves, have empathy toward others, speak and write articulately, solve problems, and be healthy and well. Schools need to be as enthusiastic about peace studies and conflict resolution programs as they are about Junior Reserve Officers' Training Corps (JROTC) programs. Schools should include time each day for discussion topics like cosmopolitanism, their country's constitution, and the Universal Declaration of Human Rights.

ESTABLISH A DEPARTMENT OF PEACE AT THE NATIONAL LEVEL

It is clear that military force and our policy of preemption are alone insufficient to make us safe. But help is on the way. Legislation has been proposed to create a US Department of Peace. In the proposed Department of Peace it would organize our present system into one conscious effort to improve humanity in achieving peace, where true safety lies.

—WALTER CRONKITE

The establishment of a Department of Peace would send a message to the world that the US is serious about peace. Funds would be provided for research on best practices, and peacemaking and peacebuilding (building long-term and sustainable pathways) would be a central element of planning instead of total reliance on peacekeeping (curtailing hostilities). Prevention would have a high priority as well as dealing effectively with the root causes of war. This would involve a cabinet position that further heightens the value of seeking and achieving authentic peace in the world rather than the kind of peace that has been defined as a lull between wars. Instead of being tied to the idea of "wars of the future," we can begin to envision a peace of the future. Department status would enable our society to fund research and peacemaking interventions that promote healing and reconciliation. At present, we are very lopsided on the side of war with an enormous military-industrial-intelligence complex that consumes a significant part of our annual budget and has not brought peace and social justice but rather an increase in the number of people in the world who would do us harm. A Department of Peace would help turn the US from a culture of war to a culture of peace—a most worthy pursuit.

INCLUDE ANIMAL RIGHTS AND ECOLOGY IN SCHOOL CURRICULA

The human spirit is not dead. It lives on in secret. . . . It has come to believe that compassion, in which all ethics must take root, can only attain its full breadth and depth if it embraces all living creatures and does not limit itself to mankind.

—ALBERT SCHWEITZER

Animal rights and the environment are appropriate subjects for school curricula because they affect our values and health. For example, animals raised in factory farms are denied adequate space, light, movement, and sufficient parent–offspring bonding. These sentient creatures are also injected with chemicals to prevent the spread of diseases caused by close quarter confinement. These chemicals remain in the animals after they are processed for human consumption at which time they become carcinogens. Factory-farmed meat is both unhealthy and immoral, diminishing the moral fiber of human beings who become complicit in animal cruelty.

The waste products of these factories contribute significantly to air, water pollution, and deforestation. These farms use an inordinate amount of water that the world is running short of, and the grain used to feed these animals could contribute to famine-impacted populations around the world. Students need an informed understanding of how their eating habits intersect with ethics and human and ecological health. Shielding students from that knowledge to preserve the status quo constitutes dishonesty. Errors of omission promote distrust within students. Animals are sentient beings and deserve basic rights. If given full information, students could become leaders in exploring alternative ways to feed the people on the planet without resorting to cruel and inhumane methods that diminish our own humanity.

ESTABLISH MULLER'S WORLD CORE CURRICULUM IN ALL SCHOOLS

In the final analysis . . . the main function of education is to make children happy, fulfilled, universal human beings.

—ROBERT MULLER

Perhaps the most important vehicle for achieving authentic and lasting peace and social justice is global education. Robert Muller's World Core Curriculum, discussed earlier, exemplifies the best attempt to provide a global perspective for all children in the world. The perspectives provided in the curriculum are far reaching and could do much to extend knowledge about our diverse world and the commonalities people on earth share. This curriculum would open minds and hearts and bring people together as fellow sojourners on this planet. It would help break down barriers and promote the kind of mutual acceptance that can pave the way for a kinder and more empathetic world.

CONVERSION FROM REPRESENTATIVE TO PARTICIPATORY DEMOCRACY

The most effective way to revive a functional democracy is to do what we have always done; transfer decision-making from the unaccountable institutions: monarchs, priestly castes, military juntas, political or economic dictatorships, or modern corporations, and bring it back to the public arena.

—AARON NORDQUIST

Too often, representative democracy does not address the needs of ordinary people. In a representative democracy, those who are eligible to vote elect people to represent them as senators and congresspeople who are meant to heed the desires of the voters who placed them in office. The supposed goal of the representative is to try to balance all the different desires of their constituency, keeping in mind the greatest good for the greatest number. However, there is no guarantee that constituent interests are central to decision-making, particularly when special interest groups spend huge amounts of money to elect those aspiring to get into or remain in office. Such interest groups expect something in return. Since it requires large sums of money to run for office, many of those running for office are wealthy and accrue greater wealth during their time in office. Those who are skeptical of the ethics underlying this system sometimes point to the large number of congresspeople who leave congress with millions of dollars in net worth, far above the return of typical investments. The mere appearance of this situation is enough to call it into serious question.

In a participatory, or direct, democracy, every citizen plays an active role in government. Of course, this requires an informed citizenry, but the very existence of such a structure would encourage citizens to become more informed and active because they know their votes would have a direct impact on policy. When people have a direct say in what impacts them, they often rise to the occasion. Authentic democracy promotes buy-in. Too many decisions are made in government that have little to do with what citizens need or want. Corporate interests appear to trump all. With participatory democracy, there would be much more debate on issues, and voters would have to vote thoughtfully. The level of thinking would rise and with it the kind of policies and laws that do not place the interests of the wealthy over the needs of ordinary citizens.

LEAD WITH PEACEBUILDING, NOT MILITARY INTERVENTION

Where military force has been employed intervention is needed before anger hardens into bitterness, revenge and retaliation.

—SCILLA ELWORTHY

Anytime a country uses unilateral military force with stated benign intent, there is always a question of whether that country is acting primarily on self-interest. Military intervention, even when taken in an effort to stop a genocide or halt hostilities in a civil war, often creates a political vacuum for warring factions to regroup or in which hostile groups stop fighting but remain mutually suspicious of each other. Peacekeeping has great limitations because it relies mainly on force, and force is an external control that resists internalization. It is a lot like spanking children, which stops an undesirable behavior momentarily but does little to change motives or behavior removed from the immediate threat. Children who are spanked learn to be sneaky and manipulative. When they are in places where spanking is not imminent, they tend to repeat undesirable behaviors.

When military missions and peacekeeping forces have completed their work, they often leave behind unfinished work that can only be finished by peacebuilders who focus on conflict resolution, trust-building, communication, forgiveness, healing, and reconciliation. The goal of peacemakers is long-term peace and social justice as well as the prevention of future conflict. Each peacekeeping intervention should include a peacemaking dimension so that when the former is phased out, the latter is phased in. Sharon D. Welch, in her 2008 book *Real Peace, Real Security: The Challenges of Global Citizenship,* provides an excellent blueprint for achieving the kind peacebuilding needed to prevent and successfully resolve international conflicts. For example, she distinguished among peacekeeping, peacemaking, and peacebuilding, and carefully describes the process of moving through them. Another book that aids greatly in understanding the steps to ensure a peaceful and just world is *A Blueprint for Achieving Peace on Earth* by Russell E. Hill, which identifies the main reasons for human conflict as well a detailed plan for the abolition of war.

Unless we try to limit the use of military force instead of using it as a first or only resort, we will continue to experience violence and war within and among countries. We must employ all the techniques and skills of which human beings are capable and not just those destructive means that continue the cycles of human and environmental degradation.

Bibliography

Ackerman, Peter, and Jack Duvall. *A Force More Powerful: A Century of Nonviolent Conflict*. 1st Palgrave ed. New York: Palgrave, 2001.

Alliance for Peacebuilding. "What We Do." https://www.allianceforpeacebuilding.org/what-we-do.

Arms Control Association. "The Nuclear Proliferation Treaty (NPT) at a Glance." https://www.armscontrol.org/factsheets/nptfact.

Barash, David P. *Approaches to Peace: A Reader in Peace Studies*. 3rd ed. Oxford: Oxford University Press, 2014.

Barash, David P., and Charles Webel. *Peace and Conflict Studies*. 5th ed. Thousand Oaks, CA: Sage, 2021.

Barr, John. "We Are Abolishing War." Unpublished manuscript, 1995.

Beller, Ken, and Heather Chase. *Great Peacemakers: True Stories from Around the World*. Sedona, AZ: LTS, 2008.

Breaking the Silence. "About." https://www.breakingthesilence.org.il/about/organization.

Brown, Charles J. "Ambassador for All War Crimes Except Our Own." *Huffington Post*, Sept. 22, 2008.

Buber, Martin. *Pointing the Way*. New York: Harper & Row, 1962.

Çaltekin, Demet Aslı. *Conscientious Objection in Turkey: A Socio-Legal Analysis of the Right to Refuse Military Service*. Edinburgh: Edinburgh University Press, 2022.

Chawkins, Steve. "Garry Davis Dies at 91; World Citizen No. 1 and Advocate for Peace." *Los Angeles Times*, Apr. 1, 2013.

Chenoweth, Erica, and Maria J. Stephan. *Why Civil Resistance Works: The Strategic Logic of Nonviolent Conflict*. New York: Columbia University Press, 2011. http://public.ebookcentral.proquest.com/choice/publicfullrecord.aspx?p=908815.

Clark, Grenville, and Louis B. Sohn. *World Peace Through World Law*. 2nd ed. Cambridge: Harvard University Press, 1962.

CODEPINK. "What Is CODEPINK?" https://www.codepink.org/about.

Cortright, David. *Peace: A History of Movements and Ideas*. Cambridge: Cambridge University Press, 2008.

———, ed. *Truth Seekers: Voices of Peace and Nonviolence from Gandhi to Pope Francis*. Maryknoll, NY: Orbis, 2020.

Davis, Garry. "The History of Gary Davis." http://www.garrydavis.org/history.

Einstein, Albert. *The Expanded Quotable Einstein*. Edited by Alice Calaprice. Princeton: Princeton University Press, 2000.

Ely, Elissa. "The Remembrance Project: Colonel John Barr." WBUR, July 4, 2015. https://www.wbur.org/the-remembrance-project/2015/07/04/the-remembrance-project-colonel-john-barr.

Epstein, Joyce Levy. *School, Family, and Community Partnerships: Preparing Educators and Improving Schools*. 2nd ed. Boulder, CO: Westview Press, 2011.

Evangelista, Matthew. *Unarmed Forces: The Transnational Movement to End the Cold War*. Ithaca, NY: Cornell University Press, 1999.

Fahey, Joseph. *War and the Christian Conscience: Where Do You Stand?* Maryknoll, NY: Orbis, 2005.

Kristensen, Hans, et al. "Status of World Nuclear Forces." Federation of American Scientists, Mar. 26, 2025. https://fas.org/initiative/status-world-nuclear-forces/.

Fisher, Roger, and William Ury. *Getting to Yes: Negotiating Agreement Without Giving In*. Edited by Bruce Patton. 3rd rev. ed. New York: Penguin, 2011.

Freire, Paulo. *Pedagogy of the Oppressed*. 30th anniversary ed. New York: Continuum, 2000.

Fromm, Erich. *On Being Human*. London: The Continuum International Publishing Group, 1997.

Galtung, Johan. *Peace by Peaceful Means: Peace and Conflict, Development and Civilization*. London: Sage, 1996. http://site.ebrary.com/id/10369641.

Galtung, Johan, et al. *Searching for Peace: The Road to Transcend*. Sterling, VA: Pluto, 2002.

Gandhi. *The Gandhi Reader: A Source Book of His Life and Writings*. Edited by Homer A. Jack. 1st Evergreen ed. New York: Grove Press, 1956.

Garthoff, Raymond L. Review of *The ABCs of the Soviet-American Nuclear Arms Race*, by Ray Perkins, Jr. *Political Science Quarterly* 106 (1991) 334–35. https://doi.org/10.2307/2152245.

Genesio, Jerry. *Veterans for Peace: The First Decade*. Falmouth, ME: Pequawket, 1997.

GI Rights Network. "About." https://www.girightshotline.org/en/about/.

Giroux, Henry. "Lessons from Paulo Freire." *Chronicle of Higher Education* 57 (2010) 1–6.

Global Action to Prevent War. "About." https://gapwblog.wordpress.com/about/.

Global Zero. "Road Map to Zero." https://www.globalzero.org/reaching-zero/index.html.

Gordon, Haim, and Leonard Grob, eds. *Education for Peace: Testimonies from World Religions*. Maryknoll, NY: Orbis, 1987.

Greene, Ashley. "You Will Have to Look for Us in Pictures: The Plight of Myanmar's Muslims." Burma Human Rights Network, forthcoming. https://bhrn.org.uk/en/report.html.

Greene, Ashley, and Ashad Sentongo. "Assessing National Mechanisms for Atrocity Prevention in Africa's Great Lakes Region." *Journal of Peacebuilding and Development* 14 (2019) 193–205.

Halberstam, Malvina. "The Right to Self-Defense Once the Security Council Takes Action." *Michigan Journal of International Law* 17 (1996). https://repository.law.umich.edu/mjil/vol17/iss2/2.

Hayner, Priscilla. *Unspeakable Truths: Transitional Justice and the Challenge of Truth Commissions*. 2nd ed. New York: Routledge, 2010.

Hill, Russell E. *A Blueprint for Achieving Peace on Earth*. CreateSpace, 2011.

Hinde, Robert, and Joseph Rotblat. *War No More*. Sterling, VA: Pluto, 2003.

History Skills. "Why Did the Catholic Church Declare a Ban on Crossbows in the Middle Ages?" https://www.historyskills.com/classroom/year-8/church-crossbow-ban/?srsltid=AfmBOooj4CDOuvJ8_-d1vJxLiY8eymZDyflrH8nym1bNbWjAqsB7yhBM.

Hitler, Adolf. *Mein Kampf.* Translated by Ralph Manheim. Boston: Houghton Mifflin, 1943.

Holmes, Robert L. *Nonviolence in Theory and Practice.* 2nd ed. Long Grove, IL: Waveland, 2005.

Holt, Robert R. "Can Psychology Meet Einstein's Challenge?" *Political Psychology* 5 (1984) 199–225. https://doi.org/10.2307/3791187.

———. "Meeting Einstein's Challenge: New Thinking About Nuclear Weapons." *Bulletin of the Atomic Scientists*, Apr. 3, 2015. https://thebulletin.org/2015/04/meeting-einsteins-challenge-new-thinking-about-nuclear-weapons/.

International Labour Organization. "ILO Constitution." Dec., 4, 2024. https://www.ilo.org/resource/other/ilo-constitution.

IPPNW. "Radioactive Heaven and Earth: The Health and Environmental Effects of Nuclear Weapons Testing in, on, and Above the Earth." *Choice Reviews Online* 29 (1992) 29–3338.

Kirkland, Allegra. "The Planet's 10 Most (and Least) Peaceful Countries. *Salon*, Aug. 12, 2014. https://www.salon.com/2014/08/12/the_planets_most_and_least_peaceful_countries_partner/.

Kramer, Mattea. "How Much Foreign Aid Does the U.S. Give Away?" *National Priorities Project*, May 6, 2013. https://www.nationalpriorities.org/blog/2013/05/06/how-much-foreign-aid-does-us-give-away/.

Kroc Institute for International Peace Studies. "Strategic Peacebuilding." https://kroc.nd.edu/research/strategic-peacebuilding/.

Lackey, Douglas P. *The Ethics of War and Peace.* Englewood Cliffs, NJ: Prentice Hall, 1989.

Lee, Thomas. *Battlebabble: Selling War in America: A Dictionary of Deception.* Monroe, ME: Common Courage, 2005.

Molineu, Harold. Review of *One World or None: A History of the World Nuclear Disarmament Movement Through* 1953, by Lawrence S. Wittner. *The Annals of the American Academy of Political and Social Science* 539 (1995) 186–87.

Morris, Errol, dir. *The Fog of War*. New York: Radical Media, 2003.

Mortimer, Edward. "The First 70 Years of the United Nations: Achievements and Challenges." *UN Chronicle*, Sept. 15, 2015. https://www.un.org/en/chronicle/article/first-70-years-united-nations-achievements-and-challenges.

Moses, A. Dirk. "Fit for Purpose? The Concept of Genocide and Civilian Destruction." In *Genocide: Key Themes*. Edited by Donald Bloxham and A. Dirk Moses, 12–44. Oxford: Oxford University Press, 2022.

Munro, Lyle. *Man Is the Cruelest Animal: Essays on the Human-Animal Link*. Champaign, IL: Common Ground Research Networks, 2021.

The National WWI Museum and Memorial. "The Fourteen Points: Woodrow Wilson and the U.S. Rejection of the Treaty of Versailles." https://www.theworldwar.org/learn/peace/fourteen-points.

The National WWII Museum. "The Cost of War." https://www.nationalww2museum.org/war/articles/cost-victory.

NATO. "'The Atlantic Charter.'" https://www.nato.int/cps/en/natohq/official_texts_16912.htm.

an-Nawawi, Yahya ibn Sharaf. *Riyad as-Salihin*. https://sunnah.com/riyadussalihin.

Nibert, David Alan. *Animal Rights/Human Rights: Entanglements of Oppression and Liberation*. Lanham, MD: Rowman & Littlefield, 2002. http://site.ebrary.com/id/10915884.

The Nobel Prize. "The Man Behind the Prize—Alfred Nobel." https://www.nobelprize.org/alfred-nobel.

———. "The Nobel Peace Prize." https://www.nobelprize.org/prizes/peace/.

Nussbaum, Martha C. *For Love of Country?* Boston: Beacon, 2002.

Ober, Frank B. "The Connally Reservation and National Security." *American Bar Association Journal* 47 (1961) 63–67.

OLL. "Did Bastiat Say 'When Goods Don't Cross Borders, Soldiers Will'?" https://oll.libertyfund.org/pages/did-bastiat-say-when-goods-don-t-cross-borders-soldiers-will.

One Country. "The Hague Centenary: Towards a Culture of Peace." http://www.onecountry.org/e103/e10302as.htm.

Oppenheimer, Mark. "A Campaign Pitch Rekindles the Question: Just What Is Liberation Theology?" *New York Times*, May 25, 2012.

Owen, John. *Of the Mortification of Sin in Believers; The Necessity, Nature, and Means of It; With a Resolution of Sundry Cases of Conscience Thereunto Belonging*. Vol. 6 of *The Works of John Owen*. Edited by William H. Goold. Edinburgh: T&T Clark, 1862.

Paul, Catherine A. "Jane Addams (1860–1935)." *VCU Social Welfare History Project.* https://socialwelfare.library.vcu.edu/settlement-houses/addams-jane/.

Perkins, Ray, and Leo R. Sandy. "The Nature of Peace and Its Implications for Peace Education." *OJPCR: The Online Journal of Peace and Conflict Resolution* 4 (2002) 1–8.

Plutarch. *Plutarch's Moralia.* Translated by Frank Cole Babbitt. London: W. Heinemann, 1927.

Ratical.org. "The McCloy/Zorin Agreement." https://ratical.org/ratville/JFK/HWNAU/MZappIX.pdf.

Reardon, Betty A. *Comprehensive Peace Education: Educating for Global Responsibility.* New York: Teachers College, Columbia University Press, 1988.

Regan, Tom, and Peter Singer. *Animal Rights and Human Obligations.* 2nd ed. Englewood Cliffs, NJ: Prentice Hall, 1989.

Rifkin, Jeremy. *The Empathic Civilization: The Race to Global Consciousness in a World in Crisis.* Cambridge: Polity Press, 2021.

Rotblat, Joseph. "If You Want Peace, Prepare for Peace." *Times Higher Education,* Nov. 29, 1996.

Rush, Benjamin. "Essays, Literary, Moral and Philosophical by Benjamin Rush, M.D. and Professor of the Institutes of Medicine and Clinical Practice in the University of Pennsylvania." In the digital collection Evans Early American Imprint Collection. University of Michigan Library Digital Collections. https://name.umdl.umich.edu/N25938.0001.001.

Russell, Bertrand, et al. "The Russell–Einstein Manifesto." International Peace Movement. https://scarc.library.oregonstate.edu/coll/pauling/peace/papers/peace6.007.5.html.

Sands, Philippe. *Lawless World: America and the Making and Breaking of Global Rules from FDR's Atlantic Charter to George W. Bush's Illegal War.* New York: Viking, 2005.

Sandy, Leo, and Scott Meyer. "Educating for Global Citizenship in the New Millennium." *The International Journal of Diversity in Organizations, Communities, and Nations: Annual Review* 9 (2009) 59–64. https://doi.org/10.18848/1447-9532/CGP/v09i01/39698.

Seathl. "Chief Seattle's Letter to All." https://www.csun.edu/~vcpsyooh/seattle.htm.

Sharp, Gene. *Civilian-Based Defense: A Post-Military Weapons System.* Princeton: Princeton University Press, 1990. https://www.nonviolent-conflict.org/wp-content/uploads/2016/02/Civilian-Based-Defense-English.pdf

———. *Exploring Nonviolent Alternatives.* Boston: Porter Sargent, 1970.

———. *Making the Abolition of War a Realistic Goal.* Cambridge, MA: Albert Einstein Institution, 1980.

———. *The Politics of Nonviolent Action.* PhD diss., St. Catherine's College, Oxford University, 1968.

Shifferd, Kent D., et al. *A Global Security System: An Alternative to War.* 5th ed. Charlottesville, VA: World Beyond War, 2020. http://public.eblib.com/choice/PublicFullRecord.aspx?p=6275620.

as-Sijistani, Abu Dawud Sulayman ibn al-Ash'ath. *Sunan Abi Dawud.* https://sunnah.com/abudawud.

Sørensen, Majken Jul, and Stellan Vinthagen. "Nonviolent Resistance and Culture." *Peace and Change* 37 (2012) 444–70. https://doi.org/10.1111/j.1468-0130.2012.00758.x.

Stiglitz, Joseph E. *The Great Divide: Unequal Societies and What We Can Do About Them.* New York: Norton & Company, 2015.

Stoner, Eric. "Pillars of Power." https://beautifultrouble.org/toolbox/tool/pillars-of-power.

Sweeney, Duane. *The Peace Catalog: A Guidebook to a Positive Future.* Los Angeles, CA: Penichet, 1984.

Thoreau, Henry David. "Resistance to Civil Government: A Lecture Delivered in 1847." In *Aesthetic Papers*, edited by Elizabeth P. Peabody. New York: G. P. Putnam, 1849.

———. *Walden.* New York: Thomas Y. Crowell, 1910. https://www.google.com/books/edition/Walden/yiQ3AAAAIAAJ?hl=en&gbpv=1&printsec=frontcover.

Ulfelder, Jay. "The Trouble with Combining, or Why I'm Not Touting the Global Peace Index." Dart-Throwing Chimp. https://dartthrowingchimp.com/2012/06/12/the-trouble-with-combining-or-why-im-not-touting-the-global-peace-index/.

UN. "Convention on the Prevention and Punishment of the Crime of Genocide." https://www.un.org/en/genocideprevention/documents/atrocity-crimes/Doc.1_Convention%20on%20the%20Prevention%20and%20Punishment%20of%20the%20Crime%20of%20Genocide.pdf.

———. "Declaration and Programme of Action on a Culture of Peace." https://www.refworld.org/legal/resolution/unga/1999/en/12411.

———. "International Law and Justice." Global Issues. https://www.un.org/en/global-issues/international-law-and-justice.

———. "United Nations Charter, Chapter 1: Purposes and Principles." https://www.un.org/en/about-us/un-charter/chapter-1#:~:text=To%20achieve%20international%20co%2Doperation,%2C%20language%2C%20or%20religion;%20and.

———. "Universal Declaration of Human Rights." https://www.un.org/en/about-us/universal-declaration-of-human-rights.

UN General Assembly. Resolution 52/13, Culture of Peace, A/RES/52/13 (Jan. 15, 1998). https://docs.un.org/en/A/RES/52/13.

US Department of State Archive. "Gorbachev and New Thinking in Soviet Foreign Policy, 1987–88." https://2001-2009.state.gov/r/pa/ho/time/rd/108225.htm.

Veterans for Peace. "Who We Are." https://gapwblog.wordpress.com/about/.

Vietnam Veterans Against the War. "About." http://www.vvaw.org/about/.

Wallensteen, Peter. *Understanding Conflict Resolution*. 6th ed. Los Angeles: Sage, 2023.

Wai Lin, Phyo, et al. "Armed Buddhists, Including Monks, Clash with Muslims in Myanmar." CNN World, Mar. 22, 2013. https://edition.cnn.com/2013/03/22/world/asia/myanmar-clashes.

Waller, James. *Confronting Evil: Engaging our Responsibility to Prevent Genocide*. New York: Oxford University Press, 2016.

Welch, Sharon D. *Real Peace, Real Security: The Challenges of Global Citizenship*. Minneapolis: Fortress, 2008.

Wittner, Lawrence S. "Einstein's Postwar Campaign to Save the World from Nuclear Destruction." *Foreign Policy in Focus*, Mar. 1, 2024. https://fpif.org/einsteins-postwar-campaign-to-save-the-world-from-nuclear-destruction/.

———. *One World or None*. Vol. 1 of *The Struggle Against the Bomb: A History of the World Nuclear Disarmament Movement Through* 1953. Stanford, CA: Stanford University Press, 1993.

The White House. "'Islam Is Peace' Says President." https://georgewbush-whitehouse.archives.gov/news/releases/2001/09/20010917-11.html.

World Beyond War. "About." https://worldbeyondwar.org/who/.

BIBLIOGRAPHY